Twelfth Night
or
What You Will

By Edward de Vere

Art:
Portrait of Edward de Vere
17th Earl of Oxford (1550-1604)

This edition produced by
Verus Publishing

www.verusbooks.com

Copyright 2019 Verus Publishing
This book, with the exception of the text of the play itself, remains the copyrighted property of the publisher and may not be duplicated or redistributed in whole or in part without express permission.

ISBN: 978-1-951267-35-3
Imprint / Publisher: Verus Publishing

The Author

Edward de Vere, 17th Earl of Oxford

Biography and Bibliography
After the Play

A Preverse

Drone on ye learned scholars of the day
As to with whom the words ahead the credit lay.
For our part though can be no further doubt
That the author of these words has been found out
To be a person lordly and refined
On whom the light of wit so boldly shined
That to keep this wit from tearing in the fray
He gave another, lesser wit his say.

Now let the least of wits
That writes these paltry lines
Yield to him whose peerless name
Should be with reverence spake.
Let this name be not of history's misassigns
Whose pen and verse have made the earth to shake.

Twelfth Night
Twelfth Night
or
What You Will

By Edward de Vere

The Main Characters

Viola – A shipwrecked young woman who disguises herself as "Cesario"

Sebastian – Viola's twin brother

Duke Orsino – Duke of Illyria

Olivia – Wealthy countess

Malvolio – A steward of Olivia

Maria – Woman of Olivia

Sir Toby Belch – Uncle of Olivia

Sir Andrew Aguecheek – Friend of Sir Toby

Feste – A jester and servant of Olivia

Fabian – Also Olivia's servant

Antonio – A sea captain & friend to Sebastian
Valentine and Curio – The Duke's attendants
Sea Captain – Friend to Viola

And now, the Play...

ACT I

SCENE I.
DUKE ORSINO's palace.

Enter DUKE ORSINO, CURIO, and other Lords; Musicians attending

DUKE ORSINO
  If music be the food of love, play on;
  Give me excess of it, that, surfeiting,
  The appetite may sicken, and so die.
  That strain again! it had a dying fall:
  O, it came o'er my ear like the sweet sound,
  That breathes upon a bank of violets,
  Stealing and giving odour! Enough; no more:
  'Tis not so sweet now as it was before.
  O spirit of love! how quick and fresh art thou,
  That, notwithstanding thy capacity
  Receiveth as the sea, nought enters there,
  Of what validity and pitch soe'er,
  But falls into abatement and low price,
  Even in a minute: so full of shapes is fancy
  That it alone is high fantastical.
CURIO
  Will you go hunt, my lord?
DUKE ORSINO
  What, Curio?
CURIO
  The hart.
DUKE ORSINO
  Why, so I do, the noblest that I have:
  O, when mine eyes did see Olivia first,
  Methought she purged the air of pestilence!

Twelfth Night – Act I

That instant was I turn'd into a hart;
And my desires, like fell and cruel hounds,
E'er since pursue me.

Enter VALENTINE

How now! what news from her?
VALENTINE
So please my lord, I might not be admitted;
But from her handmaid do return this answer:
The element itself, till seven years' heat,
Shall not behold her face at ample view;
But, like a cloistress, she will veiled walk
And water once a day her chamber round
With eye-offending brine: all this to season
A brother's dead love, which she would keep fresh
And lasting in her sad remembrance.
DUKE ORSINO
O, she that hath a heart of that fine frame
To pay this debt of love but to a brother,
How will she love, when the rich golden shaft
Hath kill'd the flock of all affections else
That live in her; when liver, brain and heart,
These sovereign thrones, are all supplied, and fill'd
Her sweet perfections with one self king!
Away before me to sweet beds of flowers:
Love-thoughts lie rich when canopied with bowers.

Exeunt

Twelfth Night — Act I

SCENE II.

The sea-coast.

Enter VIOLA, a Captain, and Sailors

VIOLA
What country, friends, is this?
Captain
This is Illyria, lady.
VIOLA
And what should I do in Illyria?
My brother he is in Elysium.
Perchance he is not drown'd: what think you, sailors?
Captain
It is perchance that you yourself were saved.
VIOLA
O my poor brother! and so perchance may he be.
Captain
True, madam: and, to comfort you with chance,
Assure yourself, after our ship did split,
When you and those poor number saved with you
Hung on our driving boat, I saw your brother,
Most provident in peril, bind himself,
Courage and hope both teaching him the practise,
To a strong mast that lived upon the sea;
Where, like Arion on the dolphin's back,
I saw him hold acquaintance with the waves
So long as I could see.
VIOLA
For saying so, there's gold:
Mine own escape unfoldeth to my hope,
Whereto thy speech serves for authority,
The like of him. Know'st thou this country?
Captain
Ay, madam, well; for I was bred and born

Not three hours' travel from this very place.
VIOLA
Who governs here?
Captain
A noble duke, in nature as in name.
VIOLA
What is the name?
Captain
Orsino.
VIOLA
Orsino! I have heard my father name him:
He was a bachelor then.
Captain
And so is now, or was so very late;
For but a month ago I went from hence,
And then 'twas fresh in murmur,--as, you know,
What great ones do the less will prattle of,--
That he did seek the love of fair Olivia.
VIOLA
What's she?
Captain
A virtuous maid, the daughter of a count
That died some twelvemonth since, then leaving her
In the protection of his son, her brother,
Who shortly also died: for whose dear love,
They say, she hath abjured the company
And sight of men.
VIOLA
O that I served that lady
And might not be delivered to the world,
Till I had made mine own occasion mellow,
What my estate is!
Captain
That were hard to compass;

Twelfth Night — Act I

Because she will admit no kind of suit,
No, not the duke's.

VIOLA
There is a fair behavior in thee, captain;
And though that nature with a beauteous wall
Doth oft close in pollution, yet of thee
I will believe thou hast a mind that suits
With this thy fair and outward character.
I prithee, and I'll pay thee bounteously,
Conceal me what I am, and be my aid
For such disguise as haply shall become
The form of my intent. I'll serve this duke:
Thou shall present me as an eunuch to him:
It may be worth thy pains; for I can sing
And speak to him in many sorts of music
That will allow me very worth his service.
What else may hap to time I will commit;
Only shape thou thy silence to my wit.

Captain
Be you his eunuch, and your mute I'll be:
When my tongue blabs, then let mine eyes not see.

VIOLA
I thank thee: lead me on.

Exeunt

SCENE III.

OLIVIA'S house.

Enter SIR TOBY BELCH and MARIA

SIR TOBY BELCH
What a plague means my niece, to take the death of
her brother thus? I am sure care's an enemy to life.

MARIA

By my troth, Sir Toby, you must come in earlier o'
nights: your cousin, my lady, takes great
exceptions to your ill hours.
SIR TOBY BELCH
Why, let her except, before excepted.
MARIA
Ay, but you must confine yourself within the modest
limits of order.
SIR TOBY BELCH
Confine! I'll confine myself no finer than I am:
these clothes are good enough to drink in; and so be
these boots too: an they be not, let them hang
themselves in their own straps.
MARIA
That quaffing and drinking will undo you: I heard
my lady talk of it yesterday; and of a foolish
knight that you brought in one night here to be her
wooer.
SIR TOBY BELCH
Who, Sir Andrew Aguecheek?
MARIA
Ay, he.
SIR TOBY BELCH
He's as tall a man as any's in Illyria.
MARIA
What's that to the purpose?
SIR TOBY BELCH
Why, he has three thousand ducats a year.
MARIA
Ay, but he'll have but a year in all these ducats:
he's a very fool and a prodigal.
SIR TOBY BELCH
Fie, that you'll say so! he plays o' the
viol-de-gamboys, and speaks three or four languages

Twelfth Night — Act I

word for word without book, and hath all the good gifts of nature.

MARIA
He hath indeed, almost natural: for besides that he's a fool, he's a great quarreller: and but that he hath the gift of a coward to allay the gust he hath in quarrelling, 'tis thought among the prudent he would quickly have the gift of a grave.

SIR TOBY BELCH
By this hand, they are scoundrels and subtractors that say so of him. Who are they?

MARIA
They that add, moreover, he's drunk nightly in your company.

SIR TOBY BELCH
With drinking healths to my niece: I'll drink to her as long as there is a passage in my throat and drink in Illyria: he's a coward and a coystrill that will not drink to my niece till his brains turn o' the toe like a parish-top. What, wench! Castiliano vulgo! for here comes Sir Andrew Agueface.

Enter SIR ANDREW

SIR ANDREW
Sir Toby Belch! how now, Sir Toby Belch!

SIR TOBY BELCH
Sweet Sir Andrew!

SIR ANDREW
Bless you, fair shrew.

MARIA
And you too, sir.

SIR TOBY BELCH
Accost, Sir Andrew, accost.

SIR ANDREW

Twelfth Night — Act I

What's that?
SIR TOBY BELCH
My niece's chambermaid.
SIR ANDREW
Good Mistress Accost, I desire better acquaintance.
MARIA
My name is Mary, sir.
SIR ANDREW
Good Mistress Mary Accost,--
SIR TOBY BELCH
You mistake, knight; 'accost' is front her, board her, woo her, assail her.
SIR ANDREW
By my troth, I would not undertake her in this company. Is that the meaning of 'accost'?
MARIA
Fare you well, gentlemen.
SIR TOBY BELCH
An thou let part so, Sir Andrew, would thou mightst never draw sword again.
SIR ANDREW
An you part so, mistress, I would I might never draw sword again. Fair lady, do you think you have fools in hand?
MARIA
Sir, I have not you by the hand.
SIR ANDREW
Marry, but you shall have; and here's my hand.
MARIA
Now, sir, 'thought is free:' I pray you, bring your hand to the buttery-bar and let it drink.
SIR ANDREW
Wherefore, sweet-heart? what's your metaphor?
MARIA

It's dry, sir.
SIR ANDREW
Why, I think so: I am not such an ass but I can keep my hand dry. But what's your jest?
MARIA
A dry jest, sir.
SIR ANDREW
Are you full of them?
MARIA
Ay, sir, I have them at my fingers' ends: marry, now I let go your hand, I am barren.

Exit

SIR TOBY BELCH
O knight thou lackest a cup of canary: when did I see thee so put down?
SIR ANDREW
Never in your life, I think; unless you see canary put me down. Methinks sometimes I have no more wit than a Christian or an ordinary man has: but I am a great eater of beef and I believe that does harm to my wit.
SIR TOBY BELCH
No question.
SIR ANDREW
An I thought that, I'ld forswear it. I'll ride home to-morrow, Sir Toby.
SIR TOBY BELCH
Pourquoi, my dear knight?
SIR ANDREW
What is 'Pourquoi'? do or not do? I would I had bestowed that time in the tongues that I have in fencing, dancing and bear-baiting: O, had I but followed the arts!

Twelfth Night — Act I

SIR TOBY BELCH
  Then hadst thou had an excellent head of hair.
SIR ANDREW
  Why, would that have mended my hair?
SIR TOBY BELCH
  Past question; for thou seest it will not curl by nature.
SIR ANDREW
  But it becomes me well enough, does't not?
SIR TOBY BELCH
  Excellent; it hangs like flax on a distaff; and I
  hope to see a housewife take thee between her legs
  and spin it off.
SIR ANDREW
  Faith, I'll home to-morrow, Sir Toby: your niece
  will not be seen; or if she be, it's four to one
  she'll none of me: the count himself here hard by woos
  her.
SIR TOBY BELCH
  She'll none o' the count: she'll not match above
  her degree, neither in estate, years, nor wit; I
  have heard her swear't. Tut, there's life in't,
  man.
SIR ANDREW
  I'll stay a month longer. I am a fellow o' the
  strangest mind i' the world; I delight in masques
  and revels sometimes altogether.
SIR TOBY BELCH
  Art thou good at these kickshawses, knight?
SIR ANDREW
  As any man in Illyria, whatsoever he be, under the
  degree of my betters; and yet I will not compare
  with an old man.
SIR TOBY BELCH
  What is thy excellence in a galliard, knight?

SIR ANDREW

Faith, I can cut a caper.

SIR TOBY BELCH

And I can cut the mutton to't.

SIR ANDREW

And I think I have the back-trick simply as strong as any man in Illyria.

SIR TOBY BELCH

Wherefore are these things hid? wherefore have these gifts a curtain before 'em? are they like to take dust, like Mistress Mall's picture? why dost thou not go to church in a galliard and come home in a coranto? My very walk should be a jig; I would not so much as make water but in a sink-a-pace. What dost thou mean? Is it a world to hide virtues in? I did think, by the excellent constitution of thy leg, it was formed under the star of a galliard.

SIR ANDREW

Ay, 'tis strong, and it does indifferent well in a flame-coloured stock. Shall we set about some revels?

SIR TOBY BELCH

What shall we do else? were we not born under Taurus?

SIR ANDREW

Taurus! That's sides and heart.

SIR TOBY BELCH

No, sir; it is legs and thighs. Let me see the caper; ha! higher: ha, ha! excellent!

Exeunt

Twelfth Night — Act I

SCENE IV.
DUKE ORSINO's palace.

Enter VALENTINE and VIOLA in man's attire

VALENTINE
If the duke continue these favours towards you, Cesario, you are like to be much advanced: he hath known you but three days, and already you are no stranger.

VIOLA
You either fear his humour or my negligence, that you call in question the continuance of his love: is he inconstant, sir, in his favours?

VALENTINE
No, believe me.

VIOLA
I thank you. Here comes the count.

Enter DUKE ORSINO, CURIO, and Attendants

DUKE ORSINO
Who saw Cesario, ho?

VIOLA
On your attendance, my lord; here.

DUKE ORSINO
Stand you a while aloof, Cesario,
Thou know'st no less but all; I have unclasp'd
To thee the book even of my secret soul:
Therefore, good youth, address thy gait unto her;
Be not denied access, stand at her doors,
And tell them, there thy fixed foot shall grow
Till thou have audience.

VIOLA
Sure, my noble lord,
If she be so abandon'd to her sorrow
As it is spoke, she never will admit me.

Twelfth Night — Act I

DUKE ORSINO
Be clamorous and leap all civil bounds
Rather than make unprofited return.

VIOLA
Say I do speak with her, my lord, what then?

DUKE ORSINO
O, then unfold the passion of my love,
Surprise her with discourse of my dear faith:
It shall become thee well to act my woes;
She will attend it better in thy youth
Than in a nuncio's of more grave aspect.

VIOLA
I think not so, my lord.

DUKE ORSINO
Dear lad, believe it;
For they shall yet belie thy happy years,
That say thou art a man: Diana's lip
Is not more smooth and rubious; thy small pipe
Is as the maiden's organ, shrill and sound,
And all is semblative a woman's part.
I know thy constellation is right apt
For this affair. Some four or five attend him;
All, if you will; for I myself am best
When least in company. Prosper well in this,
And thou shalt live as freely as thy lord,
To call his fortunes thine.

VIOLA
I'll do my best
To woo your lady:

Aside

yet, a barful strife!
Whoe'er I woo, myself would be his wife.

Exeunt

Twelfth Night — Act I

SCENE V.

OLIVIA'S house.

Enter MARIA and Clown

MARIA
   Nay, either tell me where thou hast been, or I will not open my lips so wide as a bristle may enter in way of thy excuse: my lady will hang thee for thy absence.

Clown
   Let her hang me: he that is well hanged in this world needs to fear no colours.

MARIA
   Make that good.

Clown
   He shall see none to fear.

MARIA
   A good lenten answer: I can tell thee where that saying was born, of 'I fear no colours.'

Clown
   Where, good Mistress Mary?

MARIA
   In the wars; and that may you be bold to say in your foolery.

Clown
   Well, God give them wisdom that have it; and those that are fools, let them use their talents.

MARIA
   Yet you will be hanged for being so long absent; or, to be turned away, is not that as good as a hanging to you?

Clown
   Many a good hanging prevents a bad marriage; and, for turning away, let summer bear it out.

Twelfth Night — Act I

MARIA
> You are resolute, then?

Clown
> Not so, neither; but I am resolved on two points.

MARIA
> That if one break, the other will hold; or, if both break, your gaskins fall.

Clown
> Apt, in good faith; very apt. Well, go thy way; if Sir Toby would leave drinking, thou wert as witty a piece of Eve's flesh as any in Illyria.

MARIA
> Peace, you rogue, no more o' that. Here comes my lady: make your excuse wisely, you were best.

Exit

Clown
> Wit, an't be thy will, put me into good fooling! Those wits, that think they have thee, do very oft prove fools; and I, that am sure I lack thee, may pass for a wise man: for what says Quinapalus? 'Better a witty fool, than a foolish wit.'

Enter OLIVIA with MALVOLIO

> God bless thee, lady!

OLIVIA
> Take the fool away.

Clown
> Do you not hear, fellows? Take away the lady.

OLIVIA
> Go to, you're a dry fool; I'll no more of you: besides, you grow dishonest.

Clown

Twelfth Night — Act I

Two faults, madonna, that drink and good counsel
will amend: for give the dry fool drink, then is
the fool not dry: bid the dishonest man mend
himself; if he mend, he is no longer dishonest; if
he cannot, let the botcher mend him. Any thing
that's mended is but patched: virtue that
transgresses is but patched with sin; and sin that
amends is but patched with virtue. If that this
simple syllogism will serve, so; if it will not,
what remedy? As there is no true cuckold but
calamity, so beauty's a flower. The lady bade take
away the fool; therefore, I say again, take her away.

OLIVIA

Sir, I bade them take away you.

Clown

Misprision in the highest degree! Lady, cucullus non
facit monachum; that's as much to say as I wear not
motley in my brain. Good madonna, give me leave to
prove you a fool.

OLIVIA

Can you do it?

Clown

Dexterously, good madonna.

OLIVIA

Make your proof.

Clown

I must catechise you for it, madonna: good my mouse
of virtue, answer me.

OLIVIA

Well, sir, for want of other idleness, I'll bide your proof.

Clown

Good madonna, why mournest thou?

OLIVIA

Good fool, for my brother's death.

Twelfth Night — Act I

Clown
I think his soul is in hell, madonna.
OLIVIA
I know his soul is in heaven, fool.
Clown
The more fool, madonna, to mourn for your brother's soul being in heaven. Take away the fool, gentlemen.
OLIVIA
What think you of this fool, Malvolio? doth he not mend?
MALVOLIO
Yes, and shall do till the pangs of death shake him: infirmity, that decays the wise, doth ever make the better fool.
Clown
God send you, sir, a speedy infirmity, for the better increasing your folly! Sir Toby will be sworn that I am no fox; but he will not pass his word for two pence that you are no fool.
OLIVIA
How say you to that, Malvolio?
MALVOLIO
I marvel your ladyship takes delight in such a barren rascal: I saw him put down the other day with an ordinary fool that has no more brain than a stone. Look you now, he's out of his guard already; unless you laugh and minister occasion to him, he is gagged. I protest, I take these wise men, that crow so at these set kind of fools, no better than the fools' zanies.
OLIVIA
Oh, you are sick of self-love, Malvolio, and taste with a distempered appetite. To be generous, guiltless and of free disposition, is to take those

things for bird-bolts that you deem cannon-bullets:
there is no slander in an allowed fool, though he do
nothing but rail; nor no railing in a known discreet
man, though he do nothing but reprove.

Clown
> Now Mercury endue thee with leasing, for thou
> speakest well of fools!

Re-enter MARIA

MARIA
> Madam, there is at the gate a young gentleman much
> desires to speak with you.

OLIVIA
> From the Count Orsino, is it?

MARIA
> I know not, madam: 'tis a fair young man, and well
> attended.

OLIVIA
> Who of my people hold him in delay?

MARIA
> Sir Toby, madam, your kinsman.

OLIVIA
> Fetch him off, I pray you; he speaks nothing but
> madman: fie on him!

Exit MARIA

Go you, Malvolio: if it be a suit from the count, I
am sick, or not at home; what you will, to dismiss it.

Exit MALVOLIO

Now you see, sir, how your fooling grows old, and
people dislike it.

Clown

Twelfth Night — Act I

Thou hast spoke for us, madonna, as if thy eldest son should be a fool; whose skull Jove cram with brains! for,--here he comes,--one of thy kin has a most weak pia mater.

Enter SIR TOBY BELCH

OLIVIA
By mine honour, half drunk. What is he at the gate, cousin?
SIR TOBY BELCH
A gentleman.
OLIVIA
A gentleman! what gentleman?
SIR TOBY BELCH
'Tis a gentle man here--a plague o' these pickle-herring! How now, sot!
Clown
Good Sir Toby!
OLIVIA
Cousin, cousin, how have you come so early by this lethargy?
SIR TOBY BELCH
Lechery! I defy lechery. There's one at the gate.
OLIVIA
Ay, marry, what is he?
SIR TOBY BELCH
Let him be the devil, an he will, I care not: give me faith, say I. Well, it's all one.

Exit

OLIVIA
What's a drunken man like, fool?
Clown

Twelfth Night — Act I

Like a drowned man, a fool and a mad man: one
draught above heat makes him a fool; the second mads
him; and a third drowns him.

OLIVIA
Go thou and seek the crowner, and let him sit o' my
coz; for he's in the third degree of drink, he's
drowned: go, look after him.

Clown
He is but mad yet, madonna; and the fool shall look
to the madman.

Exit

Re-enter MALVOLIO

MALVOLIO
Madam, yond young fellow swears he will speak with
you. I told him you were sick; he takes on him to
understand so much, and therefore comes to speak
with you. I told him you were asleep; he seems to
have a foreknowledge of that too, and therefore
comes to speak with you. What is to be said to him,
lady? he's fortified against any denial.

OLIVIA
Tell him he shall not speak with me.

MALVOLIO
Has been told so; and he says, he'll stand at your
door like a sheriff's post, and be the supporter to
a bench, but he'll speak with you.

OLIVIA
What kind o' man is he?

MALVOLIO
Why, of mankind.

OLIVIA

Twelfth Night — Act I

What manner of man?

MALVOLIO

Of very ill manner; he'll speak with you, will you or no.

OLIVIA

Of what personage and years is he?

MALVOLIO

Not yet old enough for a man, nor young enough for a boy; as a squash is before 'tis a peascod, or a cooling when 'tis almost an apple: 'tis with him in standing water, between boy and man. He is very well-favoured and he speaks very shrewishly; one would think his mother's milk were scarce out of him.

OLIVIA

Let him approach: call in my gentlewoman.

MALVOLIO

Gentlewoman, my lady calls.

Exit

Re-enter MARIA

OLIVIA

Give me my veil: come, throw it o'er my face.
We'll once more hear Orsino's embassy.

Enter VIOLA, and Attendants

VIOLA

The honourable lady of the house, which is she?

OLIVIA

Speak to me; I shall answer for her.
Your will?

VIOLA

Most radiant, exquisite and unmatchable beauty,--I pray you, tell me if this be the lady of the house,

Twelfth Night — Act I

for I never saw her: I would be loath to cast away
my speech, for besides that it is excellently well
penned, I have taken great pains to con it. Good
beauties, let me sustain no scorn; I am very
comptible, even to the least sinister usage.

OLIVIA
Whence came you, sir?

VIOLA
I can say little more than I have studied, and that
question's out of my part. Good gentle one, give me
modest assurance if you be the lady of the house,
that I may proceed in my speech.

OLIVIA
Are you a comedian?

VIOLA
No, my profound heart: and yet, by the very fangs
of malice I swear, I am not that I play. Are you
the lady of the house?

OLIVIA
If I do not usurp myself, I am.

VIOLA
Most certain, if you are she, you do usurp
yourself; for what is yours to bestow is not yours
to reserve. But this is from my commission: I will
on with my speech in your praise, and then show you
the heart of my message.

OLIVIA
Come to what is important in't: I forgive you the praise.

VIOLA
Alas, I took great pains to study it, and 'tis poetical.

OLIVIA
It is the more like to be feigned: I pray you,
keep it in. I heard you were saucy at my gates,
and allowed your approach rather to wonder at you

than to hear you. If you be not mad, be gone; if
you have reason, be brief: 'tis not that time of
moon with me to make one in so skipping a dialogue.
MARIA
Will you hoist sail, sir? here lies your way.
VIOLA
No, good swabber; I am to hull here a little
longer. Some mollification for your giant, sweet
lady. Tell me your mind: I am a messenger.
OLIVIA
Sure, you have some hideous matter to deliver, when
the courtesy of it is so fearful. Speak your office.
VIOLA
It alone concerns your ear. I bring no overture of
war, no taxation of homage: I hold the olive in my
hand; my words are as fun of peace as matter.
OLIVIA
Yet you began rudely. What are you? what would you?
VIOLA
The rudeness that hath appeared in me have I
learned from my entertainment. What I am, and what I
would, are as secret as maidenhead; to your ears,
divinity, to any other's, profanation.
OLIVIA
Give us the place alone: we will hear this divinity.

Exeunt MARIA and Attendants

Now, sir, what is your text?
VIOLA
Most sweet lady,--
OLIVIA
A comfortable doctrine, and much may be said of it.
Where lies your text?
VIOLA

Twelfth Night — Act I

In Orsino's bosom.

OLIVIA

In his bosom! In what chapter of his bosom?

VIOLA

To answer by the method, in the first of his heart.

OLIVIA

O, I have read it: it is heresy. Have you no more to say?

VIOLA

Good madam, let me see your face.

OLIVIA

Have you any commission from your lord to negotiate
with my face? You are now out of your text: but
we will draw the curtain and show you the picture.
Look you, sir, such a one I was this present: is't
not well done?

Unveiling

VIOLA

Excellently done, if God did all.

OLIVIA

'Tis in grain, sir; 'twill endure wind and weather.

VIOLA

'Tis beauty truly blent, whose red and white
Nature's own sweet and cunning hand laid on:
Lady, you are the cruell'st she alive,
If you will lead these graces to the grave
And leave the world no copy.

OLIVIA

O, sir, I will not be so hard-hearted; I will give
out divers schedules of my beauty: it shall be
inventoried, and every particle and utensil
labelled to my will: as, item, two lips,
indifferent red; item, two grey eyes, with lids to
them; item, one neck, one chin, and so forth. Were

you sent hither to praise me?
VIOLA
I see you what you are, you are too proud;
But, if you were the devil, you are fair.
My lord and master loves you: O, such love
Could be but recompensed, though you were crown'd
The nonpareil of beauty!
OLIVIA
How does he love me?
VIOLA
With adorations, fertile tears,
With groans that thunder love, with sighs of fire.
OLIVIA
Your lord does know my mind; I cannot love him:
Yet I suppose him virtuous, know him noble,
Of great estate, of fresh and stainless youth;
In voices well divulged, free, learn'd and valiant;
And in dimension and the shape of nature
A gracious person: but yet I cannot love him;
He might have took his answer long ago.
VIOLA
If I did love you in my master's flame,
With such a suffering, such a deadly life,
In your denial I would find no sense;
I would not understand it.
OLIVIA
Why, what would you?
VIOLA
Make me a willow cabin at your gate,
And call upon my soul within the house;
Write loyal cantons of contemned love
And sing them loud even in the dead of night;
Halloo your name to the reverberate hills
And make the babbling gossip of the air

Twelfth Night — Act I

Cry out 'Olivia!' O, You should not rest
Between the elements of air and earth,
But you should pity me!

OLIVIA
You might do much.
What is your parentage?

VIOLA
Above my fortunes, yet my state is well:
I am a gentleman.

OLIVIA
Get you to your lord;
I cannot love him: let him send no more;
Unless, perchance, you come to me again,
To tell me how he takes it. Fare you well:
I thank you for your pains: spend this for me.

VIOLA
I am no fee'd post, lady; keep your purse:
My master, not myself, lacks recompense.
Love make his heart of flint that you shall love;
And let your fervor, like my master's, be
Placed in contempt! Farewell, fair cruelty.

Exit

OLIVIA
'What is your parentage?'
'Above my fortunes, yet my state is well:
I am a gentleman.' I'll be sworn thou art;
Thy tongue, thy face, thy limbs, actions and spirit,
Do give thee five-fold blazon: not too fast:
soft, soft!
Unless the master were the man. How now!
Even so quickly may one catch the plague?
Methinks I feel this youth's perfections
With an invisible and subtle stealth

To creep in at mine eyes. Well, let it be.
What ho, Malvolio!

Re-enter MALVOLIO

MALVOLIO
Here, madam, at your service.
OLIVIA
Run after that same peevish messenger,
The county's man: he left this ring behind him,
Would I or not: tell him I'll none of it.
Desire him not to flatter with his lord,
Nor hold him up with hopes; I am not for him:
If that the youth will come this way to-morrow,
I'll give him reasons for't: hie thee, Malvolio.
MALVOLIO
Madam, I will.

Exit

OLIVIA
I do I know not what, and fear to find
Mine eye too great a flatterer for my mind.
Fate, show thy force: ourselves we do not owe;
What is decreed must be, and be this so.

Exit

ACT II

SCENE I.
The sea-coast.

Enter ANTONIO and SEBASTIAN

ANTONIO
 Will you stay no longer? nor will you not that I go with you?
SEBASTIAN
 By your patience, no. My stars shine darkly over me: the malignancy of my fate might perhaps distemper yours; therefore I shall crave of you your leave that I may bear my evils alone: it were a bad recompense for your love, to lay any of them on you.
ANTONIO
 Let me yet know of you whither you are bound.
SEBASTIAN
 No, sooth, sir: my determinate voyage is mere extravagancy. But I perceive in you so excellent a touch of modesty, that you will not extort from me what I am willing to keep in; therefore it charges me in manners the rather to express myself. You must know of me then, Antonio, my name is Sebastian, which I called Roderigo. My father was that Sebastian of Messaline, whom I know you have heard of. He left behind him myself and a sister, both
 born in an hour: if the heavens had been pleased, would we had so ended! but you, sir, altered that; for some hour before you took me from the breach of the sea was my sister drowned.
ANTONIO
 Alas the day!

Twelfth Night — Act II

SEBASTIAN

A lady, sir, though it was said she much resembled
me, was yet of many accounted beautiful: but,
though I could not with such estimable wonder
overfar believe that, yet thus far I will boldly
publish her; she bore a mind that envy could not but
call fair. She is drowned already, sir, with salt
water, though I seem to drown her remembrance again
with more.

ANTONIO

Pardon me, sir, your bad entertainment.

SEBASTIAN

O good Antonio, forgive me your trouble.

ANTONIO

If you will not murder me for my love, let me be
your servant.

SEBASTIAN

If you will not undo what you have done, that is,
kill him whom you have recovered, desire it not.
Fare ye well at once: my bosom is full of kindness,
and I am yet so near the manners of my mother, that
upon the least occasion more mine eyes will tell
tales of me. I am bound to the Count Orsino's court:
farewell.

Exit

ANTONIO

The gentleness of all the gods go with thee!
I have many enemies in Orsino's court,
Else would I very shortly see thee there.
But, come what may, I do adore thee so,
That danger shall seem sport, and I will go.

Exit

Twelfth Night — Act II

SCENE II.
A street.

Enter VIOLA, MALVOLIO following

MALVOLIO
Were not you even now with the Countess Olivia?
VIOLA
Even now, sir; on a moderate pace I have since
arrived but hither.
MALVOLIO
She returns this ring to you, sir: you might have
saved me my pains, to have taken it away yourself.
She adds, moreover, that you should put your lord
into a desperate assurance she will none of him:
and one thing more, that you be never so hardy to
come again in his affairs, unless it be to report
your lord's taking of this. Receive it so.
VIOLA
She took the ring of me: I'll none of it.
MALVOLIO
Come, sir, you peevishly threw it to her; and her
will is, it should be so returned: if it be worth
stooping for, there it lies in your eye; if not, be
it his that finds it.

Exit

VIOLA
I left no ring with her: what means this lady?
Fortune forbid my outside have not charm'd her!
She made good view of me; indeed, so much,
That sure methought her eyes had lost her tongue,
For she did speak in starts distractedly.

Twelfth Night — Act II

She loves me, sure; the cunning of her passion
Invites me in this churlish messenger.
None of my lord's ring! why, he sent her none.
I am the man: if it be so, as 'tis,
Poor lady, she were better love a dream.
Disguise, I see, thou art a wickedness,
Wherein the pregnant enemy does much.
How easy is it for the proper-false
In women's waxen hearts to set their forms!
Alas, our frailty is the cause, not we!
For such as we are made of, such we be.
How will this fadge? my master loves her dearly;
And I, poor monster, fond as much on him;
And she, mistaken, seems to dote on me.
What will become of this? As I am man,
My state is desperate for my master's love;
As I am woman,--now alas the day!--
What thriftless sighs shall poor Olivia breathe!
O time! thou must untangle this, not I;
It is too hard a knot for me to untie!

Exit

SCENE III.

OLIVIA's house.

Enter SIR TOBY BELCH and SIR ANDREW

SIR TOBY BELCH
Approach, Sir Andrew: not to be abed after midnight is to be up betimes; and 'diluculo surgere,' thou know'st,--

SIR ANDREW
Nay, my troth, I know not: but I know, to be up late is to be up late.

Twelfth Night — Act II

SIR TOBY BELCH
A false conclusion: I hate it as an unfilled can.
To be up after midnight and to go to bed then, is
early: so that to go to bed after midnight is to go
to bed betimes. Does not our life consist of the
four elements?

SIR ANDREW
Faith, so they say; but I think it rather consists
of eating and drinking.

SIR TOBY BELCH
Thou'rt a scholar; let us therefore eat and drink.
Marian, I say! a stoup of wine!

Enter Clown

SIR ANDREW
Here comes the fool, i' faith.

Clown
How now, my hearts! did you never see the picture
of 'we three'?

SIR TOBY BELCH
Welcome, ass. Now let's have a catch.

SIR ANDREW
By my troth, the fool has an excellent breast. I
had rather than forty shillings I had such a leg,
and so sweet a breath to sing, as the fool has. In
sooth, thou wast in very gracious fooling last
night, when thou spokest of Pigrogromitus, of the
Vapians passing the equinoctial of Queubus: 'twas
very good, i' faith. I sent thee sixpence for thy
leman: hadst it?

Clown
I did impeticos thy gratillity; for Malvolio's nose
is no whipstock: my lady has a white hand, and the
Myrmidons are no bottle-ale houses.

Twelfth Night — Act II

SIR ANDREW
Excellent! why, this is the best fooling, when all is done. Now, a song.
SIR TOBY BELCH
Come on; there is sixpence for you: let's have a song.
SIR ANDREW
There's a testril of me too: if one knight give a--
Clown
Would you have a love-song, or a song of good life?
SIR TOBY BELCH
A love-song, a love-song.
SIR ANDREW
Ay, ay: I care not for good life.
Clown
[Sings]
O mistress mine, where are you roaming?
O, stay and hear; your true love's coming,
That can sing both high and low:
Trip no further, pretty sweeting;
Journeys end in lovers meeting,
Every wise man's son doth know.
SIR ANDREW
Excellent good, i' faith.
SIR TOBY BELCH
Good, good.
Clown
[Sings]
What is love? 'tis not hereafter;
Present mirth hath present laughter;
What's to come is still unsure:
In delay there lies no plenty;
Then come kiss me, sweet and twenty,
Youth's a stuff will not endure.
SIR ANDREW

Twelfth Night — Act II

A mellifluous voice, as I am true knight.

SIR TOBY BELCH

A contagious breath.

SIR ANDREW

Very sweet and contagious, i' faith.

SIR TOBY BELCH

To hear by the nose, it is dulcet in contagion. But shall we make the welkin dance indeed? shall we rouse the night-owl in a catch that will draw three souls out of one weaver? shall we do that?

SIR ANDREW

An you love me, let's do't: I am dog at a catch.

Clown

By'r lady, sir, and some dogs will catch well.

SIR ANDREW

Most certain. Let our catch be, 'Thou knave.'

Clown

'Hold thy peace, thou knave,' knight? I shall be constrained in't to call thee knave, knight.

SIR ANDREW

'Tis not the first time I have constrained one to call me knave. Begin, fool: it begins 'Hold thy peace.'

Clown

I shall never begin if I hold my peace.

SIR ANDREW

Good, i' faith. Come, begin.

Catch sung

Enter MARIA

MARIA

What a caterwauling do you keep here! If my lady have not called up her steward Malvolio and bid him

turn you out of doors, never trust me.
SIR TOBY BELCH
My lady's a Cataian, we are politicians, Malvolio's a Peg-a-Ramsey, and 'Three merry men be we.' Am not I consanguineous? am I not of her blood? Tillyvally. Lady!

Sings

'There dwelt a man in Babylon, lady, lady!'
Clown
Beshrew me, the knight's in admirable fooling.
SIR ANDREW
Ay, he does well enough if he be disposed, and so do I too: he does it with a better grace, but I do it more natural.
SIR TOBY BELCH
[Sings] 'O, the twelfth day of December,'--
MARIA
For the love o' God, peace!

Enter MALVOLIO

MALVOLIO
My masters, are you mad? or what are you? Have ye no wit, manners, nor honesty, but to gabble like tinkers at this time of night? Do ye make an alehouse of my lady's house, that ye squeak out your coziers' catches without any mitigation or remorse of voice? Is there no respect of place, persons, nor time in you?
SIR TOBY BELCH
We did keep time, sir, in our catches. Sneck up!
MALVOLIO
Sir Toby, I must be round with you. My lady bade me

tell you, that, though she harbours you as her kinsman, she's nothing allied to your disorders. If you can separate yourself and your misdemeanors, you are welcome to the house; if not, an it would please you to take leave of her, she is very willing to bid you farewell.

SIR TOBY BELCH
'Farewell, dear heart, since I must needs be gone.'

MARIA
Nay, good Sir Toby.

Clown
'His eyes do show his days are almost done.'

MALVOLIO
Is't even so?

SIR TOBY BELCH
'But I will never die.'

Clown
Sir Toby, there you lie.

MALVOLIO
This is much credit to you.

SIR TOBY BELCH
'Shall I bid him go?'

Clown
'What an if you do?'

SIR TOBY BELCH
'Shall I bid him go, and spare not?'

Clown
'O no, no, no, no, you dare not.'

SIR TOBY BELCH
Out o' tune, sir: ye lie. Art any more than a steward? Dost thou think, because thou art virtuous, there shall be no more cakes and ale?

Clown
Yes, by Saint Anne, and ginger shall be hot i' the

Twelfth Night — Act II

mouth too.
SIR TOBY BELCH
Thou'rt i' the right. Go, sir, rub your chain with crumbs. A stoup of wine, Maria!
MALVOLIO
Mistress Mary, if you prized my lady's favour at any thing more than contempt, you would not give means for this uncivil rule: she shall know of it, by this hand.

Exit

MARIA
Go shake your ears.
SIR ANDREW
'Twere as good a deed as to drink when a man's a-hungry, to challenge him the field, and then to break promise with him and make a fool of him.
SIR TOBY BELCH
Do't, knight: I'll write thee a challenge: or I'll deliver thy indignation to him by word of mouth.
MARIA
Sweet Sir Toby, be patient for tonight: since the youth of the count's was today with thy lady, she is much out of quiet. For Monsieur Malvolio, let me alone with him: if I do not gull him into a nayword, and make him a common recreation, do not think I have wit enough to lie straight in my bed: I know I can do it.
SIR TOBY BELCH
Possess us, possess us; tell us something of him.
MARIA
Marry, sir, sometimes he is a kind of puritan.
SIR ANDREW
O, if I thought that I'ld beat him like a dog!
SIR TOBY BELCH

What, for being a puritan? thy exquisite reason, dear knight?

SIR ANDREW
I have no exquisite reason for't, but I have reason good enough.

MARIA
The devil a puritan that he is, or any thing constantly, but a time-pleaser; an affectioned ass, that cons state without book and utters it by great swarths: the best persuaded of himself, so crammed, as he thinks, with excellencies, that it is his grounds of faith that all that look on him love him; and on that vice in him will my revenge find notable cause to work.

SIR TOBY BELCH
What wilt thou do?

MARIA
I will drop in his way some obscure epistles of love; wherein, by the colour of his beard, the shape of his leg, the manner of his gait, the expressure of his eye, forehead, and complexion, he shall find himself most feelingly personated. I can write very like my lady your niece: on a forgotten matter we can hardly make distinction of our hands.

SIR TOBY BELCH
Excellent! I smell a device.

SIR ANDREW
I have't in my nose too.

SIR TOBY BELCH
He shall think, by the letters that thou wilt drop, that they come from my niece, and that she's in love with him.

MARIA
My purpose is, indeed, a horse of that colour.

Twelfth Night — Act II

SIR ANDREW
And your horse now would make him an ass.
MARIA
Ass, I doubt not.
SIR ANDREW
O, 'twill be admirable!
MARIA
Sport royal, I warrant you: I know my physic will work with him. I will plant you two, and let the fool make a third, where he shall find the letter: observe his construction of it. For this night, to bed, and dream on the event. Farewell.

Exit

SIR TOBY BELCH
Good night, Penthesilea.
SIR ANDREW
Before me, she's a good wench.
SIR TOBY BELCH
She's a beagle, true-bred, and one that adores me: what o' that?
SIR ANDREW
I was adored once too.
SIR TOBY BELCH
Let's to bed, knight. Thou hadst need send for more money.
SIR ANDREW
If I cannot recover your niece, I am a foul way out.
SIR TOBY BELCH
Send for money, knight: if thou hast her not i' the end, call me cut.
SIR ANDREW
If I do not, never trust me, take it how you will.
SIR TOBY BELCH

Twelfth Night — Act II

Come, come, I'll go burn some sack; 'tis too late
to go to bed now: come, knight; come, knight.

Exeunt

SCENE IV.

DUKE ORSINO's palace.

Enter DUKE ORSINO, VIOLA, CURIO, and others

DUKE ORSINO
Give me some music. Now, good morrow, friends.
Now, good Cesario, but that piece of song,
That old and antique song we heard last night:
Methought it did relieve my passion much,
More than light airs and recollected terms
Of these most brisk and giddy-paced times:
Come, but one verse.

CURIO
He is not here, so please your lordship that should sing
it.

DUKE ORSINO
Who was it?

CURIO
Feste, the jester, my lord; a fool that the lady
Olivia's father took much delight in. He is about the
house.

DUKE ORSINO
Seek him out, and play the tune the while.

Exit CURIO. Music plays

Come hither, boy: if ever thou shalt love,
In the sweet pangs of it remember me;
For such as I am all true lovers are,

    Unstaid and skittish in all motions else,
    Save in the constant image of the creature
    That is beloved. How dost thou like this tune?
VIOLA
    It gives a very echo to the seat
    Where Love is throned.
DUKE ORSINO
    Thou dost speak masterly:
    My life upon't, young though thou art, thine eye
    Hath stay'd upon some favour that it loves:
    Hath it not, boy?
VIOLA
    A little, by your favour.
DUKE ORSINO
    What kind of woman is't?
VIOLA
    Of your complexion.
DUKE ORSINO
    She is not worth thee, then. What years, i' faith?
VIOLA
    About your years, my lord.
DUKE ORSINO
    Too old by heaven: let still the woman take
    An elder than herself: so wears she to him,
    So sways she level in her husband's heart:
    For, boy, however we do praise ourselves,
    Our fancies are more giddy and unfirm,
    More longing, wavering, sooner lost and worn,
    Than women's are.
VIOLA
    I think it well, my lord.
DUKE ORSINO
    Then let thy love be younger than thyself,
    Or thy affection cannot hold the bent;

Twelfth Night — Act II

    For women are as roses, whose fair flower
    Being once display'd, doth fall that very hour.
VIOLA
    And so they are: alas, that they are so;
    To die, even when they to perfection grow!

Re-enter CURIO and Clown

DUKE ORSINO
    O, fellow, come, the song we had last night.
    Mark it, Cesario, it is old and plain;
    The spinsters and the knitters in the sun
    And the free maids that weave their thread with bones
    Do use to chant it: it is silly sooth,
    And dallies with the innocence of love,
    Like the old age.
Clown
    Are you ready, sir?
DUKE ORSINO
    Ay; prithee, sing.

Music

    SONG.
Clown
    Come away, come away, death,
    And in sad cypress let me be laid;
    Fly away, fly away breath;
    I am slain by a fair cruel maid.
    My shroud of white, stuck all with yew,
    O, prepare it!
    My part of death, no one so true
    Did share it.
    Not a flower, not a flower sweet
    On my black coffin let there be strown;

Twelfth Night — Act II

    Not a friend, not a friend greet
    My poor corpse, where my bones shall be thrown:
    A thousand thousand sighs to save,
    Lay me, O, where
    Sad true lover never find my grave,
    To weep there!

DUKE ORSINO
    There's for thy pains.

Clown
    No pains, sir: I take pleasure in singing, sir.

DUKE ORSINO
    I'll pay thy pleasure then.

Clown
    Truly, sir, and pleasure will be paid, one time or another.

DUKE ORSINO
    Give me now leave to leave thee.

Clown
    Now, the melancholy god protect thee; and the tailor make thy doublet of changeable taffeta, for thy mind is a very opal. I would have men of such constancy put to sea, that their business might be every thing and their intent every where; for that's it that always makes a good voyage of nothing. Farewell.

Exit

DUKE ORSINO
    Let all the rest give place.

CURIO and Attendants retire

    Once more, Cesario,
    Get thee to yond same sovereign cruelty:
    Tell her, my love, more noble than the world,

Prizes not quantity of dirty lands;
The parts that fortune hath bestow'd upon her,
Tell her, I hold as giddily as fortune;
But 'tis that miracle and queen of gems
That nature pranks her in attracts my soul.
VIOLA
But if she cannot love you, sir?
DUKE ORSINO
I cannot be so answer'd.
VIOLA
Sooth, but you must.
Say that some lady, as perhaps there is,
Hath for your love a great a pang of heart
As you have for Olivia: you cannot love her;
You tell her so; must she not then be answer'd?
DUKE ORSINO
There is no woman's sides
Can bide the beating of so strong a passion
As love doth give my heart; no woman's heart
So big, to hold so much; they lack retention
Alas, their love may be call'd appetite,
No motion of the liver, but the palate,
That suffer surfeit, cloyment and revolt;
But mine is all as hungry as the sea,
And can digest as much: make no compare
Between that love a woman can bear me
And that I owe Olivia.
VIOLA
Ay, but I know--
DUKE ORSINO
What dost thou know?
VIOLA
Too well what love women to men may owe:
In faith, they are as true of heart as we.

  My father had a daughter loved a man,
  As it might be, perhaps, were I a woman,
  I should your lordship.
DUKE ORSINO
  And what's her history?
VIOLA
  A blank, my lord. She never told her love,
  But let concealment, like a worm i' the bud,
  Feed on her damask cheek: she pined in thought,
  And with a green and yellow melancholy
  She sat like patience on a monument,
  Smiling at grief. Was not this love indeed?
  We men may say more, swear more: but indeed
  Our shows are more than will; for still we prove
  Much in our vows, but little in our love.
DUKE ORSINO
  But died thy sister of her love, my boy?
VIOLA
  I am all the daughters of my father's house,
  And all the brothers too: and yet I know not.
  Sir, shall I to this lady?
DUKE ORSINO
  Ay, that's the theme.
  To her in haste; give her this jewel; say,
  My love can give no place, bide no denay.

Exeunt

SCENE V.

OLIVIA's garden.

Enter SIR TOBY BELCH, SIR ANDREW, and FABIAN

SIR TOBY BELCH
  Come thy ways, Signior Fabian.

Twelfth Night — Act II

FABIAN
　Nay, I'll come: if I lose a scruple of this sport,
　let me be boiled to death with melancholy.
SIR TOBY BELCH
　Wouldst thou not be glad to have the niggardly
　rascally sheep-biter come by some notable shame?
FABIAN
　I would exult, man: you know, he brought me out o'
　favour with my lady about a bear-baiting here.
SIR TOBY BELCH
　To anger him we'll have the bear again; and we will
　fool him black and blue: shall we not, Sir Andrew?
SIR ANDREW
　An we do not, it is pity of our lives.
SIR TOBY BELCH
　Here comes the little villain.

Enter MARIA

　How now, my metal of India!
MARIA
　Get ye all three into the box-tree: Malvolio's
　coming down this walk: he has been yonder i' the
　sun practising behavior to his own shadow this half
　hour: observe him, for the love of mockery; for I
　know this letter will make a contemplative idiot of
　him. Close, in the name of jesting! Lie thou there,

Throws down a letter

　for here comes the trout that must be caught with
　tickling.

Exit

Enter MALVOLIO

Twelfth Night — Act II

MALVOLIO
'Tis but fortune; all is fortune. Maria once told me she did affect me: and I have heard herself come thus near, that, should she fancy, it should be one of my complexion. Besides, she uses me with a more exalted respect than any one else that follows her. What should I think on't?

SIR TOBY BELCH
Here's an overweening rogue!

FABIAN
O, peace! Contemplation makes a rare turkey-cock of him: how he jets under his advanced plumes!

SIR ANDREW
'Slight, I could so beat the rogue!

SIR TOBY BELCH
Peace, I say.

MALVOLIO
To be Count Malvolio!

SIR TOBY BELCH
Ah, rogue!

SIR ANDREW
Pistol him, pistol him.

SIR TOBY BELCH
Peace, peace!

MALVOLIO
There is example for't; the lady of the Strachy married the yeoman of the wardrobe.

SIR ANDREW
Fie on him, Jezebel!

FABIAN
O, peace! now he's deeply in: look how imagination blows him.

MALVOLIO

Twelfth Night — Act II

Having been three months married to her, sitting in my state,--

SIR TOBY BELCH
O, for a stone-bow, to hit him in the eye!

MALVOLIO
Calling my officers about me, in my branched velvet gown; having come from a day-bed, where I have left Olivia sleeping,--

SIR TOBY BELCH
Fire and brimstone!

FABIAN
O, peace, peace!

MALVOLIO
And then to have the humour of state; and after a demure travel of regard, telling them I know my place as I would they should do theirs, to for my kinsman Toby,--

SIR TOBY BELCH
Bolts and shackles!

FABIAN
O peace, peace, peace! now, now.

MALVOLIO
Seven of my people, with an obedient start, make out for him: I frown the while; and perchance wind up watch, or play with my--some rich jewel. Toby approaches; courtesies there to me,--

SIR TOBY BELCH
Shall this fellow live?

FABIAN
Though our silence be drawn from us with cars, yet peace.

MALVOLIO
I extend my hand to him thus, quenching my familiar smile with an austere regard of control,--

Twelfth Night — Act II

SIR TOBY BELCH
And does not Toby take you a blow o' the lips then?
MALVOLIO
Saying, 'Cousin Toby, my fortunes having cast me on
your niece give me this prerogative of speech,'--
SIR TOBY BELCH
What, what?
MALVOLIO
'You must amend your drunkenness.'
SIR TOBY BELCH
Out, scab!
FABIAN
Nay, patience, or we break the sinews of our plot.
MALVOLIO
'Besides, you waste the treasure of your time with
a foolish knight,'--
SIR ANDREW
That's me, I warrant you.
MALVOLIO
'One Sir Andrew,'--
SIR ANDREW
I knew 'twas I; for many do call me fool.
MALVOLIO
What employment have we here?

Taking up the letter

FABIAN
Now is the woodcock near the gin.
SIR TOBY BELCH
O, peace! and the spirit of humour intimate reading
aloud to him!
MALVOLIO
By my life, this is my lady's hand these be her
very C's, her U's and her T's and thus makes she her

great P's. It is, in contempt of question, her hand.

SIR ANDREW

Her C's, her U's and her T's: why that?

MALVOLIO

[Reads] 'To the unknown beloved, this, and my good wishes:'--her very phrases! By your leave, wax.
Soft! and the impressure her Lucrece, with which she uses to seal: 'tis my lady. To whom should this be?

FABIAN

This wins him, liver and all.

MALVOLIO

[Reads]
Jove knows I love: But who?
Lips, do not move;
No man must know.
'No man must know.' What follows? the numbers altered! 'No man must know:' if this should be thee, Malvolio?

SIR TOBY BELCH

Marry, hang thee, brock!

MALVOLIO

[Reads]
I may command where I adore;
But silence, like a Lucrece knife,
With bloodless stroke my heart doth gore:
M, O, A, I, doth sway my life.

FABIAN

A fustian riddle!

SIR TOBY BELCH

Excellent wench, say I.

MALVOLIO

'M, O, A, I, doth sway my life.' Nay, but first, let me see, let me see, let me see.

FABIAN

Twelfth Night — Act II

What dish o' poison has she dressed him!
SIR TOBY BELCH
And with what wing the staniel cheques at it!
MALVOLIO
'I may command where I adore.' Why, she may command
me: I serve her; she is my lady. Why, this is
evident to any formal capacity; there is no
obstruction in this: and the end,--what should
that alphabetical position portend? If I could make
that resemble something in me,--Softly! M, O, A, I,--
SIR TOBY BELCH
O, ay, make up that: he is now at a cold scent.
FABIAN
Sowter will cry upon't for all this, though it be as
rank as a fox.
MALVOLIO
M,--Malvolio; M,--why, that begins my name.
FABIAN
Did not I say he would work it out? the cur is
excellent at faults.
MALVOLIO
M,--but then there is no consonancy in the sequel;
that suffers under probation A should follow but O does.
FABIAN
And O shall end, I hope.
SIR TOBY BELCH
Ay, or I'll cudgel him, and make him cry O!
MALVOLIO
And then I comes behind.
FABIAN
Ay, an you had any eye behind you, you might see
more detraction at your heels than fortunes before

you.
MALVOLIO
M, O, A, I; this simulation is not as the former: and yet, to crush this a little, it would bow to me, for every one of these letters are in my name. Soft! here follows prose.

Reads

'If this fall into thy hand, revolve. In my stars I am above thee; but be not afraid of greatness: some are born great, some achieve greatness, and some have greatness thrust upon 'em. Thy Fates open their hands; let thy blood and spirit embrace them; and, to inure thyself to what thou art like to be, cast thy humble slough and appear fresh. Be opposite with a kinsman, surly with servants; let thy tongue tang arguments of state; put thyself into the trick of singularity: she thus advises thee that sighs for thee. Remember who commended thy yellow stockings, and wished to see thee ever cross-gartered: I say, remember. Go to, thou art made, if thou desirest to be so; if not, let me see thee a steward still, the fellow of servants, and not worthy to touch Fortune's fingers. Farewell. She that would alter services with thee,
THE FORTUNATE-UNHAPPY.'
Daylight and champaign discovers not more: this is open. I will be proud, I will read politic authors, I will baffle Sir Toby, I will wash off gross acquaintance, I will be point-devise the very man. I do not now fool myself, to let imagination jade me; for every reason excites to this, that my lady loves me. She did commend my yellow stockings of late, she did praise my leg being cross-gartered;

and in this she manifests herself to my love, and with a kind of injunction drives me to these habits of her liking. I thank my stars I am happy. I will be strange, stout, in yellow stockings, and cross-gartered, even with the swiftness of putting on. Jove and my stars be praised! Here is yet a postscript.

Reads

'Thou canst not choose but know who I am. If thou entertainest my love, let it appear in thy smiling; thy smiles become thee well; therefore in my presence still smile, dear my sweet, I prithee.' Jove, I thank thee: I will smile; I will do everything that thou wilt have me.

Exit

FABIAN
I will not give my part of this sport for a pension of thousands to be paid from the Sophy.
SIR TOBY BELCH
I could marry this wench for this device.
SIR ANDREW
So could I too.
SIR TOBY BELCH
And ask no other dowry with her but such another jest.
SIR ANDREW
Nor I neither.
FABIAN
Here comes my noble gull-catcher.

Re-enter MARIA

SIR TOBY BELCH

Wilt thou set thy foot o' my neck?
SIR ANDREW
Or o' mine either?
SIR TOBY BELCH
Shall I play my freedom at traytrip, and become thy bond-slave?
SIR ANDREW
I' faith, or I either?
SIR TOBY BELCH
Why, thou hast put him in such a dream, that when the image of it leaves him he must run mad.
MARIA
Nay, but say true; does it work upon him?
SIR TOBY BELCH
Like aqua-vitae with a midwife.
MARIA
If you will then see the fruits of the sport, mark his first approach before my lady: he will come to her in yellow stockings, and 'tis a colour she abhors, and cross-gartered, a fashion she detests; and he will smile upon her, which will now be so unsuitable to her disposition, being addicted to a melancholy as she is, that it cannot but turn him into a notable contempt. If you will see it, follow me.
SIR TOBY BELCH
To the gates of Tartar, thou most excellent devil of wit!
SIR ANDREW
I'll make one too.

Exeunt

ACT III

SCENE I.

OLIVIA's garden.

Enter VIOLA, and Clown with a tabour

VIOLA
Save thee, friend, and thy music: dost thou live by
thy tabour?
Clown
No, sir, I live by the church.
VIOLA
Art thou a churchman?
Clown
No such matter, sir: I do live by the church; for
I do live at my house, and my house doth stand by
the church.
VIOLA
So thou mayst say, the king lies by a beggar, if a
beggar dwell near him; or, the church stands by thy
tabour, if thy tabour stand by the church.
Clown
You have said, sir. To see this age! A sentence is
but a cheveril glove to a good wit: how quickly the
wrong side may be turned outward!
VIOLA
Nay, that's certain; they that dally nicely with
words may quickly make them wanton.
Clown
I would, therefore, my sister had had no name, sir.
VIOLA
Why, man?
Clown

Twelfth Night — Act III

    Why, sir, her name's a word; and to dally with that
word might make my sister wanton. But indeed words
are very rascals since bonds disgraced them.

VIOLA

    Thy reason, man?

Clown

    Troth, sir, I can yield you none without words; and
words are grown so false, I am loath to prove
reason with them.

VIOLA

    I warrant thou art a merry fellow and carest for nothing.

Clown

    Not so, sir, I do care for something; but in my
conscience, sir, I do not care for you: if that be
to care for nothing, sir, I would it would make you
invisible.

VIOLA

    Art not thou the Lady Olivia's fool?

Clown

    No, indeed, sir; the Lady Olivia has no folly: she
will keep no fool, sir, till she be married; and
fools are as like husbands as pilchards are to
herrings; the husband's the bigger: I am indeed not
her fool, but her corrupter of words.

VIOLA

    I saw thee late at the Count Orsino's.

Clown

    Foolery, sir, does walk about the orb like the sun,
it shines every where. I would be sorry, sir, but
the fool should be as oft with your master as with
my mistress: I think I saw your wisdom there.

VIOLA

    Nay, an thou pass upon me, I'll no more with thee.
Hold, there's expenses for thee.

Twelfth Night — Act III

Clown
> Now Jove, in his next commodity of hair, send thee a beard!

VIOLA
> By my troth, I'll tell thee, I am almost sick for one;

Aside

> though I would not have it grow on my chin. Is thy lady within?

Clown
> Would not a pair of these have bred, sir?

VIOLA
> Yes, being kept together and put to use.

Clown
> I would play Lord Pandarus of Phrygia, sir, to bring a Cressida to this Troilus.

VIOLA
> I understand you, sir; 'tis well begged.

Clown
> The matter, I hope, is not great, sir, begging but a beggar: Cressida was a beggar. My lady is within, sir. I will construe to them whence you come; who you are and what you would are out of my welkin, I might say 'element,' but the word is over-worn.

Exit

VIOLA
> This fellow is wise enough to play the fool;
> And to do that well craves a kind of wit:
> He must observe their mood on whom he jests,
> The quality of persons, and the time,
> And, like the haggard, cheque at every feather

Twelfth Night — Act III

That comes before his eye. This is a practise
As full of labour as a wise man's art
For folly that he wisely shows is fit;
But wise men, folly-fall'n, quite taint their wit.

Enter SIR TOBY BELCH, and SIR ANDREW

SIR TOBY BELCH
Save you, gentleman.
VIOLA
And you, sir.
SIR ANDREW
Dieu vous garde, monsieur.
VIOLA
Et vous aussi; votre serviteur.
SIR ANDREW
I hope, sir, you are; and I am yours.
SIR TOBY BELCH
Will you encounter the house? my niece is desirous
you should enter, if your trade be to her.
VIOLA
I am bound to your niece, sir; I mean, she is the
list of my voyage.
SIR TOBY BELCH
Taste your legs, sir; put them to motion.
VIOLA
My legs do better understand me, sir, than I
understand what you mean by bidding me taste my legs.
SIR TOBY BELCH
I mean, to go, sir, to enter.
VIOLA
I will answer you with gait and entrance. But we
are prevented.

Enter OLIVIA and MARIA

Twelfth Night — Act III

Most excellent accomplished lady, the heavens rain odours on you!

SIR ANDREW
That youth's a rare courtier: 'Rain odours;' well.

VIOLA
My matter hath no voice, to your own most pregnant and vouchsafed ear.

SIR ANDREW
'Odours,' 'pregnant' and 'vouchsafed:' I'll get 'em all three all ready.

OLIVIA
Let the garden door be shut, and leave me to my hearing.

Exeunt SIR TOBY BELCH, SIR ANDREW, and MARIA

Give me your hand, sir.

VIOLA
My duty, madam, and most humble service.

OLIVIA
What is your name?

VIOLA
Cesario is your servant's name, fair princess.

OLIVIA
My servant, sir! 'Twas never merry world
Since lowly feigning was call'd compliment:
You're servant to the Count Orsino, youth.

VIOLA
And he is yours, and his must needs be yours:
Your servant's servant is your servant, madam.

OLIVIA
For him, I think not on him: for his thoughts,
Would they were blanks, rather than fill'd with me!

VIOLA

    Madam, I come to whet your gentle thoughts
    On his behalf.
OLIVIA
    O, by your leave, I pray you,
    I bade you never speak again of him:
    But, would you undertake another suit,
    I had rather hear you to solicit that
    Than music from the spheres.
VIOLA
    Dear lady,--
OLIVIA
    Give me leave, beseech you. I did send,
    After the last enchantment you did here,
    A ring in chase of you: so did I abuse
    Myself, my servant and, I fear me, you:
    Under your hard construction must I sit,
    To force that on you, in a shameful cunning,
    Which you knew none of yours: what might you think?
    Have you not set mine honour at the stake
    And baited it with all the unmuzzled thoughts
    That tyrannous heart can think? To one of your receiving
    Enough is shown: a cypress, not a bosom,
    Hideth my heart. So, let me hear you speak.
VIOLA
    I pity you.
OLIVIA
    That's a degree to love.
VIOLA
    No, not a grize; for 'tis a vulgar proof,
    That very oft we pity enemies.
OLIVIA
    Why, then, methinks 'tis time to smile again.
    O, world, how apt the poor are to be proud!

Twelfth Night — Act III

If one should be a prey, how much the better
To fall before the lion than the wolf!

Clock strikes

The clock upbraids me with the waste of time.
Be not afraid, good youth, I will not have you:
And yet, when wit and youth is come to harvest,
Your were is alike to reap a proper man:
There lies your way, due west.

VIOLA

Then westward-ho! Grace and good disposition
Attend your ladyship!
You'll nothing, madam, to my lord by me?

OLIVIA

Stay:
I prithee, tell me what thou thinkest of me.

VIOLA

That you do think you are not what you are.

OLIVIA

If I think so, I think the same of you.

VIOLA

Then think you right: I am not what I am.

OLIVIA

I would you were as I would have you be!

VIOLA

Would it be better, madam, than I am?
I wish it might, for now I am your fool.

OLIVIA

O, what a deal of scorn looks beautiful
In the contempt and anger of his lip!
A murderous guilt shows not itself more soon
Than love that would seem hid: love's night is noon.
Cesario, by the roses of the spring,
By maidhood, honour, truth and every thing,

I love thee so, that, maugre all thy pride,
Nor wit nor reason can my passion hide.
Do not extort thy reasons from this clause,
For that I woo, thou therefore hast no cause,
But rather reason thus with reason fetter,
Love sought is good, but given unsought better.

VIOLA
By innocence I swear, and by my youth
I have one heart, one bosom and one truth,
And that no woman has; nor never none
Shall mistress be of it, save I alone.
And so adieu, good madam: never more
Will I my master's tears to you deplore.

OLIVIA
Yet come again; for thou perhaps mayst move
That heart, which now abhors, to like his love.

Exeunt

SCENE II.

OLIVIA's house.

Enter SIR TOBY BELCH, SIR ANDREW, and FABIAN

SIR ANDREW
No, faith, I'll not stay a jot longer.

SIR TOBY BELCH
Thy reason, dear venom, give thy reason.

FABIAN
You must needs yield your reason, Sir Andrew.

SIR ANDREW
Marry, I saw your niece do more favours to the
count's serving-man than ever she bestowed upon me;
I saw't i' the orchard.

SIR TOBY BELCH

Twelfth Night — Act III

Did she see thee the while, old boy? tell me that.
SIR ANDREW
As plain as I see you now.
FABIAN
This was a great argument of love in her toward you.
SIR ANDREW
'Slight, will you make an ass o' me?
FABIAN
I will prove it legitimate, sir, upon the oaths of judgment and reason.
SIR TOBY BELCH
And they have been grand-jury-men since before Noah was a sailor.
FABIAN
She did show favour to the youth in your sight only to exasperate you, to awake your dormouse valour, to put fire in your heart and brimstone in your liver. You should then have accosted her; and with some excellent jests, fire-new from the mint, you should have banged the youth into dumbness. This was looked for at your hand, and this was balked: the double gilt of this opportunity you let time wash off, and you are now sailed into the north of my lady's opinion; where you will hang like an icicle on a Dutchman's beard, unless you do redeem it by some laudable attempt either of valour or policy.
SIR ANDREW
An't be any way, it must be with valour; for policy I hate: I had as lief be a Brownist as a politician.
SIR TOBY BELCH
Why, then, build me thy fortunes upon the basis of valour. Challenge me the count's youth to fight with him; hurt him in eleven places: my niece shall

take note of it; and assure thyself, there is no love-broker in the world can more prevail in man's commendation with woman than report of valour.

FABIAN
There is no way but this, Sir Andrew.

SIR ANDREW
Will either of you bear me a challenge to him?

SIR TOBY BELCH
Go, write it in a martial hand; be curst and brief; it is no matter how witty, so it be eloquent and fun of invention: taunt him with the licence of ink: if thou thou'st him some thrice, it shall not be amiss; and as many lies as will lie in thy sheet of paper, although the sheet were big enough for the bed of Ware in England, set 'em down: go, about it. Let there be gall enough in thy ink, though thou write with a goose-pen, no matter: about it.

SIR ANDREW
Where shall I find you?

SIR TOBY BELCH
We'll call thee at the cubiculo: go.

Exit SIR ANDREW

FABIAN
This is a dear manikin to you, Sir Toby.

SIR TOBY BELCH
I have been dear to him, lad, some two thousand strong, or so.

FABIAN
We shall have a rare letter from him: but you'll not deliver't?

SIR TOBY BELCH
Never trust me, then; and by all means stir on the youth to an answer. I think oxen and wainropes

cannot hale them together. For Andrew, if he were opened, and you find so much blood in his liver as will clog the foot of a flea, I'll eat the rest of the anatomy.
FABIAN
And his opposite, the youth, bears in his visage no great presage of cruelty.

Enter MARIA

SIR TOBY BELCH
Look, where the youngest wren of nine comes.
MARIA
If you desire the spleen, and will laugh yourself into stitches, follow me. Yond gull Malvolio is turned heathen, a very renegado; for there is no Christian, that means to be saved by believing rightly, can ever believe such impossible passages of grossness. He's in yellow stockings.
SIR TOBY BELCH
And cross-gartered?
MARIA
Most villanously; like a pedant that keeps a school i' the church. I have dogged him, like his murderer. He does obey every point of the letter that I dropped to betray him: he does smile his face into more lines than is in the new map with the augmentation of the Indies: you have not seen such a thing as 'tis. I can hardly forbear hurling things at him. I know my lady will strike him: if she do, he'll smile and take't for a great favour.
SIR TOBY BELCH
Come, bring us, bring us where he is.

Exeunt

Twelfth Night — Act III

SCENE III.
A street.

Enter SEBASTIAN and ANTONIO

SEBASTIAN
   I would not by my will have troubled you;
   But, since you make your pleasure of your pains,
   I will no further chide you.
ANTONIO
   I could not stay behind you: my desire,
   More sharp than filed steel, did spur me forth;
   And not all love to see you, though so much
   As might have drawn one to a longer voyage,
   But jealousy what might befall your travel,
   Being skilless in these parts; which to a stranger,
   Unguided and unfriended, often prove
   Rough and unhospitable: my willing love,
   The rather by these arguments of fear,
   Set forth in your pursuit.
SEBASTIAN
   My kind Antonio,
   I can no other answer make but thanks,
   And thanks; and ever [ ] oft good turns
   Are shuffled off with such uncurrent pay:
   But, were my worth as is my conscience firm,
   You should find better dealing. What's to do?
   Shall we go see the reliques of this town?
ANTONIO
   To-morrow, sir: best first go see your lodging.
SEBASTIAN
   I am not weary, and 'tis long to night:
   I pray you, let us satisfy our eyes

    With the memorials and the things of fame
    That do renown this city.
ANTONIO
    Would you'ld pardon me;
    I do not without danger walk these streets:
    Once, in a sea-fight, 'gainst the count his galleys
    I did some service; of such note indeed,
    That were I ta'en here it would scarce be answer'd.
SEBASTIAN
    Belike you slew great number of his people.
ANTONIO
    The offence is not of such a bloody nature;
    Albeit the quality of the time and quarrel
    Might well have given us bloody argument.
    It might have since been answer'd in repaying
    What we took from them; which, for traffic's sake,
    Most of our city did: only myself stood out;
    For which, if I be lapsed in this place,
    I shall pay dear.
SEBASTIAN
    Do not then walk too open.
ANTONIO
    It doth not fit me. Hold, sir, here's my purse.
    In the south suburbs, at the Elephant,
    Is best to lodge: I will bespeak our diet,
    Whiles you beguile the time and feed your knowledge
    With viewing of the town: there shall you have me.
SEBASTIAN
    Why I your purse?
ANTONIO
    Haply your eye shall light upon some toy
    You have desire to purchase; and your store,
    I think, is not for idle markets, sir.
SEBASTIAN

Twelfth Night — Act III

I'll be your purse-bearer and leave you
For an hour.
ANTONIO
To the Elephant.
SEBASTIAN
I do remember.

Exeunt

SCENE IV.
OLIVIA's garden.

Enter OLIVIA and MARIA

OLIVIA
I have sent after him: he says he'll come;
How shall I feast him? what bestow of him?
For youth is bought more oft than begg'd or borrow'd.
I speak too loud.
Where is Malvolio? he is sad and civil,
And suits well for a servant with my fortunes:
Where is Malvolio?
MARIA
He's coming, madam; but in very strange manner. He is, sure, possessed, madam.
OLIVIA
Why, what's the matter? does he rave?
MARIA
No. madam, he does nothing but smile: your ladyship were best to have some guard about you, if he come; for, sure, the man is tainted in's wits.
OLIVIA
Go call him hither.

Exit MARIA

Twelfth Night — Act III

I am as mad as he,
If sad and merry madness equal be.

Re-enter MARIA, with MALVOLIO

How now, Malvolio!
MALVOLIO
Sweet lady, ho, ho.
OLIVIA
Smilest thou?
I sent for thee upon a sad occasion.
MALVOLIO
Sad, lady! I could be sad: this does make some
obstruction in the blood, this cross-gartering; but
what of that? if it please the eye of one, it is
with me as the very true sonnet is, 'Please one, and
please all.'
OLIVIA
Why, how dost thou, man? what is the matter with thee?
MALVOLIO
Not black in my mind, though yellow in my legs. It
did come to his hands, and commands shall be
executed: I think we do know the sweet Roman hand.
OLIVIA
Wilt thou go to bed, Malvolio?
MALVOLIO
To bed! ay, sweet-heart, and I'll come to thee.
OLIVIA
God comfort thee! Why dost thou smile so and kiss
thy hand so oft?
MARIA
How do you, Malvolio?
MALVOLIO
At your request! yes; nightingales answer daws.

MARIA
  Why appear you with this ridiculous boldness before my lady?
MALVOLIO
  'Be not afraid of greatness:' 'twas well writ.
OLIVIA
  What meanest thou by that, Malvolio?
MALVOLIO
  'Some are born great,'--
OLIVIA
  Ha!
MALVOLIO
  'Some achieve greatness,'--
OLIVIA
  What sayest thou?
MALVOLIO
  'And some have greatness thrust upon them.'
OLIVIA
  Heaven restore thee!
MALVOLIO
  'Remember who commended thy yellow stocking s,'--
OLIVIA
  Thy yellow stockings!
MALVOLIO
  'And wished to see thee cross-gartered.'
OLIVIA
  Cross-gartered!
MALVOLIO
  'Go to thou art made, if thou desirest to be so;'--
OLIVIA
  Am I made?
MALVOLIO
  'If not, let me see thee a servant still.'
OLIVIA

Twelfth Night — Act III

Why, this is very midsummer madness.

Enter Servant

Servant
Madam, the young gentleman of the Count Orsino's is returned: I could hardly entreat him back: he attends your ladyship's pleasure.

OLIVIA
I'll come to him.

Exit Servant

Good Maria, let this fellow be looked to. Where's my cousin Toby? Let some of my people have a special care of him: I would not have him miscarry for the half of my dowry.

Exeunt OLIVIA and MARIA

MALVOLIO
O, ho! do you come near me now? no worse man than Sir Toby to look to me! This concurs directly with the letter: she sends him on purpose, that I may appear stubborn to him; for she incites me to that in the letter. 'Cast thy humble slough,' says she; 'be opposite with a kinsman, surly with servants; let thy tongue tang with arguments of state; put thyself into the trick of singularity;' and consequently sets down the manner how; as, a sad face, a reverend carriage, a slow tongue, in the habit of some sir of note, and so forth. I have limed her; but it is Jove's doing, and Jove make me thankful! And when she went away now, 'Let this fellow be looked to:' fellow! not Malvolio, nor after my degree, but fellow. Why, every thing

Twelfth Night — Act III

adheres together, that no dram of a scruple, no
scruple of a scruple, no obstacle, no incredulous
or unsafe circumstance--What can be said? Nothing
that can be can come between me and the full
prospect of my hopes. Well, Jove, not I, is the
doer of this, and he is to be thanked.

Re-enter MARIA, with SIR TOBY BELCH and FABIAN

SIR TOBY BELCH
Which way is he, in the name of sanctity? If all
the devils of hell be drawn in little, and Legion
himself possessed him, yet I'll speak to him.

FABIAN
Here he is, here he is. How is't with you, sir?
how is't with you, man?

MALVOLIO
Go off; I discard you: let me enjoy my private: go
off.

MARIA
Lo, how hollow the fiend speaks within him! did not
I tell you? Sir Toby, my lady prays you to have a
care of him.

MALVOLIO
Ah, ha! does she so?

SIR TOBY BELCH
Go to, go to; peace, peace; we must deal gently
with him: let me alone. How do you, Malvolio? how
is't with you? What, man! defy the devil:
consider, he's an enemy to mankind.

MALVOLIO
Do you know what you say?

MARIA
La you, an you speak ill of the devil, how he takes
it at heart! Pray God, he be not bewitched!

Twelfth Night — Act III

FABIAN
Carry his water to the wise woman.
MARIA
Marry, and it shall be done to-morrow morning, if I live. My lady would not lose him for more than I'll say.
MALVOLIO
How now, mistress!
MARIA
O Lord!
SIR TOBY BELCH
Prithee, hold thy peace; this is not the way: do you not see you move him? let me alone with him.
FABIAN
No way but gentleness; gently, gently: the fiend is rough, and will not be roughly used.
SIR TOBY BELCH
Why, how now, my bawcock! how dost thou, chuck?
MALVOLIO
Sir!
SIR TOBY BELCH
Ay, Biddy, come with me. What, man! 'tis not for gravity to play at cherry-pit with Satan: hang him, foul collier!
MARIA
Get him to say his prayers, good Sir Toby, get him to pray.
MALVOLIO
My prayers, minx!
MARIA
No, I warrant you, he will not hear of godliness.
MALVOLIO
Go, hang yourselves all! you are idle shallow things: I am not of your element: you shall know more hereafter.

Twelfth Night — Act III

Exit

SIR TOBY BELCH
Is't possible?
FABIAN
If this were played upon a stage now, I could condemn it as an improbable fiction.
SIR TOBY BELCH
His very genius hath taken the infection of the device, man.
MARIA
Nay, pursue him now, lest the device take air and taint.
FABIAN
Why, we shall make him mad indeed.
MARIA
The house will be the quieter.
SIR TOBY BELCH
Come, we'll have him in a dark room and bound. My niece is already in the belief that he's mad: we may carry it thus, for our pleasure and his penance, till our very pastime, tired out of breath, prompt us to have mercy on him: at which time we will bring the device to the bar and crown thee for a finder of madmen. But see, but see.

Enter SIR ANDREW

FABIAN
More matter for a May morning.
SIR ANDREW
Here's the challenge, read it: warrant there's vinegar and pepper in't.
FABIAN
Is't so saucy?
SIR ANDREW

Twelfth Night — Act III

Ay, is't, I warrant him: do but read.
SIR TOBY BELCH
Give me.

Reads

'Youth, whatsoever thou art, thou art but a scurvy fellow.'
FABIAN
Good, and valiant.
SIR TOBY BELCH
[Reads] 'Wonder not, nor admire not in thy mind, why I do call thee so, for I will show thee no reason for't.'
FABIAN
A good note; that keeps you from the blow of the law.
SIR TOBY BELCH
[Reads] 'Thou comest to the lady Olivia, and in my sight she uses thee kindly: but thou liest in thy throat; that is not the matter I challenge thee for.'
FABIAN
Very brief, and to exceeding good sense--less.
SIR TOBY BELCH
[Reads] 'I will waylay thee going home; where if it be thy chance to kill me,'--
FABIAN
Good.
SIR TOBY BELCH
[Reads] 'Thou killest me like a rogue and a villain.'
FABIAN
Still you keep o' the windy side of the law: good.
SIR TOBY BELCH
[Reads] 'Fare thee well; and God have mercy upon one of our souls! He may have mercy upon mine; but my hope is better, and so look to thyself. Thy

Twelfth Night – Act III

friend, as thou usest him, and thy sworn enemy,
ANDREW AGUECHEEK.
If this letter move him not, his legs cannot:
I'll give't him.

MARIA
> You may have very fit occasion for't: he is now in some commerce with my lady, and will by and by depart.

SIR TOBY BELCH
> Go, Sir Andrew: scout me for him at the corner the orchard like a bum-baily: so soon as ever thou seest him, draw; and, as thou drawest swear horrible; for it comes to pass oft that a terrible oath, with a swaggering accent sharply twanged off, gives manhood more approbation than ever proof itself would have earned him. Away!

SIR ANDREW
> Nay, let me alone for swearing.

Exit

SIR TOBY BELCH
> Now will not I deliver his letter: for the behavior of the young gentleman gives him out to be of good capacity and breeding; his employment between his lord and my niece confirms no less: therefore this letter, being so excellently ignorant, will breed no terror in the youth: he will find it comes from a clodpole. But, sir, I will deliver his challenge by word of mouth; set upon Aguecheek a notable report of valour; and drive the gentleman, as I know his youth will aptly receive it, into a most hideous opinion of his rage, skill, fury and impetuosity. This will so fright them both that they will kill one another by the look, like cockatrices.

Twelfth Night — Act III

Re-enter OLIVIA, with VIOLA

FABIAN
Here he comes with your niece: give them way till he take leave, and presently after him.
SIR TOBY BELCH
I will meditate the while upon some horrid message for a challenge.

Exeunt SIR TOBY BELCH, FABIAN, and MARIA

OLIVIA
I have said too much unto a heart of stone
And laid mine honour too unchary out:
There's something in me that reproves my fault;
But such a headstrong potent fault it is,
That it but mocks reproof.
VIOLA
With the same 'havior that your passion bears
Goes on my master's grief.
OLIVIA
Here, wear this jewel for me, 'tis my picture;
Refuse it not; it hath no tongue to vex you;
And I beseech you come again to-morrow.
What shall you ask of me that I'll deny,
That honour saved may upon asking give?
VIOLA
Nothing but this; your true love for my master.
OLIVIA
How with mine honour may I give him that
Which I have given to you?
VIOLA
I will acquit you.
OLIVIA
Well, come again to-morrow: fare thee well:

Twelfth Night — Act III

A fiend like thee might bear my soul to hell.

Exit

Re-enter SIR TOBY BELCH and FABIAN

SIR TOBY BELCH
Gentleman, God save thee.
VIOLA
And you, sir.
SIR TOBY BELCH
That defence thou hast, betake thee to't: of what nature the wrongs are thou hast done him, I know not; but thy intercepter, full of despite, bloody as the hunter, attends thee at the orchard-end: dismount thy tuck, be yare in thy preparation, for thy assailant is quick, skilful and deadly.
VIOLA
You mistake, sir; I am sure no man hath any quarrel to me: my remembrance is very free and clear from any image of offence done to any man.
SIR TOBY BELCH
You'll find it otherwise, I assure you: therefore, if you hold your life at any price, betake you to your guard; for your opposite hath in him what youth, strength, skill and wrath can furnish man withal.
VIOLA
I pray you, sir, what is he?
SIR TOBY BELCH
He is knight, dubbed with unhatched rapier and on carpet consideration; but he is a devil in private brawl: souls and bodies hath he divorced three; and his incensement at this moment is so implacable, that satisfaction can be none but by pangs of death

Twelfth Night — Act III

and sepulchre. Hob, nob, is his word; give't or take't.
VIOLA
I will return again into the house and desire some
conduct of the lady. I am no fighter. I have heard
of some kind of men that put quarrels purposely on
others, to taste their valour: belike this is a man
of that quirk.
SIR TOBY BELCH
Sir, no; his indignation derives itself out of a
very competent injury: therefore, get you on and
give him his desire. Back you shall not to the
house, unless you undertake that with me which with
as much safety you might answer him: therefore, on,
or strip your sword stark naked; for meddle you
must, that's certain, or forswear to wear iron about you.
VIOLA
This is as uncivil as strange. I beseech you, do me
this courteous office, as to know of the knight what
my offence to him is: it is something of my
negligence, nothing of my purpose.
SIR TOBY BELCH
I will do so. Signior Fabian, stay you by this
gentleman till my return.

Exit

VIOLA
Pray you, sir, do you know of this matter?
FABIAN
I know the knight is incensed against you, even to a
mortal arbitrement; but nothing of the circumstance
more.
VIOLA
I beseech you, what manner of man is he?
FABIAN

Twelfth Night — Act III

Nothing of that wonderful promise, to read him by his form, as you are like to find him in the proof of his valour. He is, indeed, sir, the most skilful, bloody and fatal opposite that you could possibly have found in any part of Illyria. Will you walk towards him? I will make your peace with him if I can.

VIOLA
I shall be much bound to you for't: I am one that had rather go with sir priest than sir knight: I care not who knows so much of my mettle.

Exeunt

Re-enter SIR TOBY BELCH, with SIR ANDREW

SIR TOBY BELCH
Why, man, he's a very devil; I have not seen such a firago. I had a pass with him, rapier, scabbard and all, and he gives me the stuck in with such a mortal motion, that it is inevitable; and on the answer, he pays you as surely as your feet hit the ground they step on. They say he has been fencer to the Sophy.

SIR ANDREW
Pox on't, I'll not meddle with him.

SIR TOBY BELCH
Ay, but he will not now be pacified: Fabian can scarce hold him yonder.

SIR ANDREW
Plague on't, an I thought he had been valiant and so cunning in fence, I'ld have seen him damned ere I'ld have challenged him. Let him let the matter slip, and I'll give him my horse, grey Capilet.

SIR TOBY BELCH

Twelfth Night — Act III

I'll make the motion: stand here, make a good show
on't: this shall end without the perdition of souls.

Aside

Marry, I'll ride your horse as well as I ride you.

Re-enter FABIAN and VIOLA

To FABIAN

I have his horse to take up the quarrel:
I have persuaded him the youth's a devil.
FABIAN
He is as horribly conceited of him; and pants and
looks pale, as if a bear were at his heels.
SIR TOBY BELCH
[To VIOLA] There's no remedy, sir; he will fight
with you for's oath sake: marry, he hath better
bethought him of his quarrel, and he finds that now
scarce to be worth talking of: therefore draw, for
the supportance of his vow; he protests he will not hurt
you.
VIOLA
[Aside] Pray God defend me! A little thing would
make me tell them how much I lack of a man.
FABIAN
Give ground, if you see him furious.
SIR TOBY BELCH
Come, Sir Andrew, there's no remedy; the gentleman
will, for his honour's sake, have one bout with you;
he cannot by the duello avoid it: but he has
promised me, as he is a gentleman and a soldier, he
will not hurt you. Come on; to't.
SIR ANDREW

Twelfth Night — Act III

Pray God, he keep his oath!
VIOLA
I do assure you, 'tis against my will.

They draw

Enter ANTONIO

ANTONIO
Put up your sword. If this young gentleman
Have done offence, I take the fault on me:
If you offend him, I for him defy you.
SIR TOBY BELCH
You, sir! why, what are you?
ANTONIO
One, sir, that for his love dares yet do more
Than you have heard him brag to you he will.
SIR TOBY BELCH
Nay, if you be an undertaker, I am for you.

They draw

Enter Officers

FABIAN
O good Sir Toby, hold! here come the officers.
SIR TOBY BELCH
I'll be with you anon.
VIOLA
Pray, sir, put your sword up, if you please.
SIR ANDREW
Marry, will I, sir; and, for that I promised you,
I'll be as good as my word: he will bear you easily
and reins well.
First Officer

Twelfth Night — Act III

    This is the man; do thy office.
Second Officer
    Antonio, I arrest thee at the suit of Count Orsino.
ANTONIO
    You do mistake me, sir.
First Officer
    No, sir, no jot; I know your favour well,
    Though now you have no sea-cap on your head.
    Take him away: he knows I know him well.
ANTONIO
    I must obey.

To VIOLA

    This comes with seeking you:
    But there's no remedy; I shall answer it.
    What will you do, now my necessity
    Makes me to ask you for my purse? It grieves me
    Much more for what I cannot do for you
    Than what befalls myself. You stand amazed;
    But be of comfort.
Second Officer
    Come, sir, away.
ANTONIO
    I must entreat of you some of that money.
VIOLA
    What money, sir?
    For the fair kindness you have show'd me here,
    And, part, being prompted by your present trouble,
    Out of my lean and low ability
    I'll lend you something: my having is not much;
    I'll make division of my present with you:
    Hold, there's half my coffer.
ANTONIO
    Will you deny me now?

Twelfth Night — Act III

    Is't possible that my deserts to you
    Can lack persuasion? Do not tempt my misery,
    Lest that it make me so unsound a man
    As to upbraid you with those kindnesses
    That I have done for you.
VIOLA
    I know of none;
    Nor know I you by voice or any feature:
    I hate ingratitude more in a man
    Than lying, vainness, babbling, drunkenness,
    Or any taint of vice whose strong corruption
    Inhabits our frail blood.
ANTONIO
    O heavens themselves!
Second Officer
    Come, sir, I pray you, go.
ANTONIO
    Let me speak a little. This youth that you see here
    I snatch'd one half out of the jaws of death,
    Relieved him with such sanctity of love,
    And to his image, which methought did promise
    Most venerable worth, did I devotion.
First Officer
    What's that to us? The time goes by: away!
ANTONIO
    But O how vile an idol proves this god
    Thou hast, Sebastian, done good feature shame.
    In nature there's no blemish but the mind;
    None can be call'd deform'd but the unkind:
    Virtue is beauty, but the beauteous evil
    Are empty trunks o'erflourish'd by the devil.
First Officer
    The man grows mad: away with him! Come, come, sir.
ANTONIO

Twelfth Night — Act III

Lead me on.

Exit with Officers

VIOLA
Methinks his words do from such passion fly,
That he believes himself: so do not I.
Prove true, imagination, O, prove true,
That I, dear brother, be now ta'en for you!
SIR TOBY BELCH
Come hither, knight; come hither, Fabian: we'll
whisper o'er a couplet or two of most sage saws.
VIOLA
He named Sebastian: I my brother know
Yet living in my glass; even such and so
In favour was my brother, and he went
Still in this fashion, colour, ornament,
For him I imitate: O, if it prove,
Tempests are kind and salt waves fresh in love.

Exit

SIR TOBY BELCH
A very dishonest paltry boy, and more a coward than
a hare: his dishonesty appears in leaving his
friend here in necessity and denying him; and for
his cowardship, ask Fabian.
FABIAN
A coward, a most devout coward, religious in it.
SIR ANDREW
'Slid, I'll after him again and beat him.
SIR TOBY BELCH
Do; cuff him soundly, but never draw thy sword.
SIR ANDREW
An I do not,--

Twelfth Night — Act III

FABIAN
  Come, let's see the event.
SIR TOBY BELCH
  I dare lay any money 'twill be nothing yet.

Exeunt

ACT IV

SCENE I.
Before OLIVIA's house.

Enter SEBASTIAN and Clown

Clown
  Will you make me believe that I am not sent for you?
SEBASTIAN
  Go to, go to, thou art a foolish fellow:
  Let me be clear of thee.
Clown
  Well held out, i' faith! No, I do not know you; nor
  I am not sent to you by my lady, to bid you come
  speak with her; nor your name is not Master Cesario;
  nor this is not my nose neither. Nothing that is so is so.
SEBASTIAN
  I prithee, vent thy folly somewhere else: Thou
  know'st not me.
Clown
  Vent my folly! he has heard that word of some
  great man and now applies it to a fool. Vent my
  folly! I am afraid this great lubber, the world,
  will prove a cockney. I prithee now, ungird thy
  strangeness and tell me what I shall vent to my
  lady: shall I vent to her that thou art coming?
SEBASTIAN
  I prithee, foolish Greek, depart from me: There's
  money for thee: if you tarry longer, I shall give
  worse payment.
Clown
  By my troth, thou hast an open hand. These wise men
  that give fools money get themselves a good

Twelfth Night — Act IV

report--after fourteen years' purchase.

Enter SIR ANDREW, SIR TOBY BELCH, and FABIAN

SIR ANDREW
Now, sir, have I met you again? there's for you.
SEBASTIAN
Why, there's for thee, and there, and there. Are all the people mad?
SIR TOBY BELCH
Hold, sir, or I'll throw your dagger o'er the house.
Clown
This will I tell my lady straight: I would not be in some of your coats for two pence.

Exit

SIR TOBY BELCH
Come on, sir; hold.
SIR ANDREW
Nay, let him alone: I'll go another way to work with him; I'll have an action of battery against him, if there be any law in Illyria: though I struck him first, yet it's no matter for that.
SEBASTIAN
Let go thy hand.
SIR TOBY BELCH
Come, sir, I will not let you go. Come, my young soldier, put up your iron: you are well fleshed; come on.
SEBASTIAN
I will be free from thee. What wouldst thou now? If thou darest tempt me further, draw thy sword.
SIR TOBY BELCH
What, what? Nay, then I must have an ounce or two of this malapert blood from you.

Enter OLIVIA

Twelfth Night — Act IV

OLIVIA
  Hold, Toby; on thy life I charge thee, hold!
SIR TOBY BELCH
  Madam!
OLIVIA
  Will it be ever thus? Ungracious wretch,
  Fit for the mountains and the barbarous caves,
  Where manners ne'er were preach'd! out of my sight!
  Be not offended, dear Cesario.
  Rudesby, be gone!
  Exeunt SIR TOBY BELCH, SIR ANDREW, and FABIAN

  I prithee, gentle friend,
  Let thy fair wisdom, not thy passion, sway
  In this uncivil and thou unjust extent
  Against thy peace. Go with me to my house,
  And hear thou there how many fruitless pranks
  This ruffian hath botch'd up, that thou thereby
  Mayst smile at this: thou shalt not choose but go:
  Do not deny. Beshrew his soul for me,
  He started one poor heart of mine in thee.
SEBASTIAN
  What relish is in this? how runs the stream?
  Or I am mad, or else this is a dream:
  Let fancy still my sense in Lethe steep;
  If it be thus to dream, still let me sleep!
OLIVIA
  Nay, come, I prithee; would thou'ldst be ruled by me!
SEBASTIAN
  Madam, I will.
OLIVIA
  O, say so, and so be!
  Exeunt

Twelfth Night — Act IV

SCENE II.
OLIVIA's house.

Enter MARIA and Clown

MARIA
Nay, I prithee, put on this gown and this beard; make him believe thou art Sir Topas the curate: do it quickly; I'll call Sir Toby the whilst.

Exit

Clown
Well, I'll put it on, and I will dissemble myself in't; and I would I were the first that ever dissembled in such a gown. I am not tall enough to become the function well, nor lean enough to be thought a good student; but to be said an honest man and a good housekeeper goes as fairly as to say a careful man and a great scholar. The competitors enter.

Enter SIR TOBY BELCH and MARIA

SIR TOBY BELCH
Jove bless thee, master Parson.

Clown
Bonos dies, Sir Toby: for, as the old hermit of Prague, that never saw pen and ink, very wittily said to a niece of King Gorboduc, 'That that is is;' so I, being Master Parson, am Master Parson; for, what is 'that' but 'that,' and 'is' but 'is'?

SIR TOBY BELCH
To him, Sir Topas.

Clown

Twelfth Night — Act IV

What, ho, I say! peace in this prison!
SIR TOBY BELCH
The knave counterfeits well; a good knave.
MALVOLIO
[Within] Who calls there?
Clown
Sir Topas the curate, who comes to visit Malvolio the lunatic.
MALVOLIO
Sir Topas, Sir Topas, good Sir Topas, go to my lady.
Clown
Out, hyperbolical fiend! how vexest thou this man! talkest thou nothing but of ladies?
SIR TOBY BELCH
Well said, Master Parson.
MALVOLIO
Sir Topas, never was man thus wronged: good Sir Topas, do not think I am mad: they have laid me here in hideous darkness.
Clown
Fie, thou dishonest Satan! I call thee by the most modest terms; for I am one of those gentle ones that will use the devil himself with courtesy: sayest thou that house is dark?
MALVOLIO
As hell, Sir Topas.
Clown
Why it hath bay windows transparent as barricadoes, and the clearstores toward the south north are as lustrous as ebony; and yet complainest thou of obstruction?
MALVOLIO
I am not mad, Sir Topas: I say to you, this house is dark.
Clown

Twelfth Night — Act IV

Madman, thou errest: I say, there is no darkness
but ignorance; in which thou art more puzzled than
the Egyptians in their fog.
MALVOLIO
I say, this house is as dark as ignorance, though
ignorance were as dark as hell; and I say, there
was never man thus abused. I am no more mad than you
are: make the trial of it in any constant question.
Clown
What is the opinion of Pythagoras concerning wild
fowl?
MALVOLIO
That the soul of our grandam might haply inhabit a bird.
Clown
What thinkest thou of his opinion?
MALVOLIO
I think nobly of the soul, and no way approve his
opinion.
Clown
Fare thee well. Remain thou still in darkness:
thou shalt hold the opinion of Pythagoras ere I will
allow of thy wits, and fear to kill a woodcock, lest
thou dispossess the soul of thy grandam. Fare thee well.
MALVOLIO
Sir Topas, Sir Topas!
SIR TOBY BELCH
My most exquisite Sir Topas!
Clown
Nay, I am for all waters.
MARIA
Thou mightst have done this without thy beard and
gown: he sees thee not.
SIR TOBY BELCH
To him in thine own voice, and bring me word how

Twelfth Night — Act IV

thou findest him: I would we were well rid of this knavery. If he may be conveniently delivered, I would he were, for I am now so far in offence with my niece that I cannot pursue with any safety this sport to the upshot. Come by and by to my chamber.

Exeunt SIR TOBY BELCH and MARIA

Clown
[Singing]
'Hey, Robin, jolly Robin,
Tell me how thy lady does.'
MALVOLIO
Fool!
Clown
'My lady is unkind, perdy.'
MALVOLIO
Fool!
Clown
'Alas, why is she so?'
MALVOLIO
Fool, I say!
Clown
'She loves another'--Who calls, ha?
MALVOLIO
Good fool, as ever thou wilt deserve well at my hand, help me to a candle, and pen, ink and paper: as I am a gentleman, I will live to be thankful to thee for't.
Clown
Master Malvolio?
MALVOLIO
Ay, good fool.
Clown
Alas, sir, how fell you besides your five wits?

Twelfth Night — Act IV

MALVOLIO
  Fool, there was never a man so notoriously abused: I am as well in my wits, fool, as thou art.
Clown
  But as well? then you are mad indeed, if you be no better in your wits than a fool.
MALVOLIO
  They have here propertied me; keep me in darkness, send ministers to me, asses, and do all they can to face me out of my wits.
Clown
  Advise you what you say; the minister is here. Malvolio, Malvolio, thy wits the heavens restore! endeavour thyself to sleep, and leave thy vain bibble babble.
MALVOLIO
  Sir Topas!
Clown
  Maintain no words with him, good fellow. Who, I, sir? not I, sir. God be wi' you, good Sir Topas. Merry, amen. I will, sir, I will.
MALVOLIO
  Fool, fool, fool, I say!
Clown
  Alas, sir, be patient. What say you sir? I am shent for speaking to you.
MALVOLIO
  Good fool, help me to some light and some paper: I tell thee, I am as well in my wits as any man in Illyria.
Clown
  Well-a-day that you were, sir
MALVOLIO
  By this hand, I am. Good fool, some ink, paper and light; and convey what I will set down to my lady:

Twelfth Night — Act IV

it shall advantage thee more than ever the bearing of letter did.

Clown
I will help you to't. But tell me true, are you not mad indeed? or do you but counterfeit?

MALVOLIO
Believe me, I am not; I tell thee true.

Clown
Nay, I'll ne'er believe a madman till I see his brains. I will fetch you light and paper and ink.

MALVOLIO
Fool, I'll requite it in the highest degree: I prithee, be gone.

Clown
[Singing]
I am gone, sir,
And anon, sir,
I'll be with you again,
In a trice,
Like to the old Vice,
Your need to sustain;
Who, with dagger of lath,
In his rage and his wrath,
Cries, ah, ha! to the devil:
Like a mad lad,
Pare thy nails, dad;
Adieu, good man devil.

Exit

Twelfth Night — Act IV

SCENE III.
OLIVIA's garden.

Enter SEBASTIAN

SEBASTIAN
This is the air; that is the glorious sun;
This pearl she gave me, I do feel't and see't;
And though 'tis wonder that enwraps me thus,
Yet 'tis not madness. Where's Antonio, then?
I could not find him at the Elephant:
Yet there he was; and there I found this credit,
That he did range the town to seek me out.
His counsel now might do me golden service;
For though my soul disputes well with my sense,
That this may be some error, but no madness,
Yet doth this accident and flood of fortune
So far exceed all instance, all discourse,
That I am ready to distrust mine eyes
And wrangle with my reason that persuades me
To any other trust but that I am mad
Or else the lady's mad; yet, if 'twere so,
She could not sway her house, command her followers,
Take and give back affairs and their dispatch
With such a smooth, discreet and stable bearing
As I perceive she does: there's something in't
That is deceiveable. But here the lady comes.

Enter OLIVIA and Priest

OLIVIA
Blame not this haste of mine. If you mean well,
Now go with me and with this holy man
Into the chantry by: there, before him,
And underneath that consecrated roof,
Plight me the full assurance of your faith;

Twelfth Night — Act IV

That my most jealous and too doubtful soul
May live at peace. He shall conceal it
Whiles you are willing it shall come to note,
What time we will our celebration keep
According to my birth. What do you say?
SEBASTIAN
I'll follow this good man, and go with you;
And, having sworn truth, ever will be true.
OLIVIA
Then lead the way, good father; and heavens so shine,
That they may fairly note this act of mine!

Exeunt

ACT V

SCENE I.
Before OLIVIA's house.
Enter Clown and FABIAN

FABIAN
Now, as thou lovest me, let me see his letter.
Clown
Good Master Fabian, grant me another request.
FABIAN
Any thing.
Clown
Do not desire to see this letter.
FABIAN
This is, to give a dog, and in recompense desire my dog again.
  Enter DUKE ORSINO, VIOLA, CURIO, and Lords

DUKE ORSINO
Belong you to the Lady Olivia, friends?
Clown
Ay, sir; we are some of her trappings.
DUKE ORSINO
I know thee well; how dost thou, my good fellow?
Clown
Truly, sir, the better for my foes and the worse for my friends.
DUKE ORSINO
Just the contrary; the better for thy friends.
Clown
No, sir, the worse.

Twelfth Night — Act V

DUKE ORSINO
  How can that be?
Clown
  Marry, sir, they praise me and make an ass of me;
  now my foes tell me plainly I am an ass: so that by
  my foes, sir I profit in the knowledge of myself,
  and by my friends, I am abused: so that,
  conclusions to be as kisses, if your four negatives
  make your two affirmatives why then, the worse for
  my friends and the better for my foes.
DUKE ORSINO
  Why, this is excellent.
Clown
  By my troth, sir, no; though it please you to be
  one of my friends.
DUKE ORSINO
  Thou shalt not be the worse for me: there's gold.
Clown
  But that it would be double-dealing, sir, I would
  you could make it another.
DUKE ORSINO
  O, you give me ill counsel.
Clown
  Put your grace in your pocket, sir, for this once,
  and let your flesh and blood obey it.
DUKE ORSINO
  Well, I will be so much a sinner, to be a
  double-dealer: there's another.
Clown
  Primo, secundo, tertio, is a good play; and the old
  saying is, the third pays for all: the triplex,
  sir, is a good tripping measure; or the bells of
  Saint Bennet, sir, may put you in mind; one, two, three.
DUKE ORSINO

Twelfth Night — Act V

You can fool no more money out of me at this throw:
if you will let your lady know I am here to speak
with her, and bring her along with you, it may awake
my bounty further.

Clown
Marry, sir, lullaby to your bounty till I come
again. I go, sir; but I would not have you to think
that my desire of having is the sin of covetousness:
but, as you say, sir, let your bounty take a nap, I
will awake it anon.

Exit

VIOLA
Here comes the man, sir, that did rescue me.

Enter ANTONIO and Officers

DUKE ORSINO
That face of his I do remember well;
Yet, when I saw it last, it was besmear'd
As black as Vulcan in the smoke of war:
A bawbling vessel was he captain of,
For shallow draught and bulk unprizable;
With which such scathful grapple did he make
With the most noble bottom of our fleet,
That very envy and the tongue of loss
Cried fame and honour on him. What's the matter?

First Officer
Orsino, this is that Antonio
That took the Phoenix and her fraught from Candy;
And this is he that did the Tiger board,
When your young nephew Titus lost his leg:
Here in the streets, desperate of shame and state,
In private brabble did we apprehend him.

Twelfth Night — Act V

VIOLA
   He did me kindness, sir, drew on my side;
   But in conclusion put strange speech upon me:
   I know not what 'twas but distraction.
DUKE ORSINO
   Notable pirate! thou salt-water thief!
   What foolish boldness brought thee to their mercies,
   Whom thou, in terms so bloody and so dear,
   Hast made thine enemies?
ANTONIO
   Orsino, noble sir,
   Be pleased that I shake off these names you give me:
   Antonio never yet was thief or pirate,
   Though I confess, on base and ground enough,
   Orsino's enemy. A witchcraft drew me hither:
   That most ingrateful boy there by your side,
   From the rude sea's enraged and foamy mouth
   Did I redeem; a wreck past hope he was:
   His life I gave him and did thereto add
   My love, without retention or restraint,
   All his in dedication; for his sake
   Did I expose myself, pure for his love,
   Into the danger of this adverse town;
   Drew to defend him when he was beset:
   Where being apprehended, his false cunning,
   Not meaning to partake with me in danger,
   Taught him to face me out of his acquaintance,
   And grew a twenty years removed thing
   While one would wink; denied me mine own purse,
   Which I had recommended to his use
   Not half an hour before.
VIOLA
   How can this be?
DUKE ORSINO

Twelfth Night — Act V

When came he to this town?
ANTONIO
To-day, my lord; and for three months before,
No interim, not a minute's vacancy,
Both day and night did we keep company.
Enter OLIVIA and Attendants

DUKE ORSINO
Here comes the countess: now heaven walks on earth.
But for thee, fellow; fellow, thy words are madness:
Three months this youth hath tended upon me;
But more of that anon. Take him aside.
OLIVIA
What would my lord, but that he may not have,
Wherein Olivia may seem serviceable?
Cesario, you do not keep promise with me.
VIOLA
Madam!
DUKE ORSINO
Gracious Olivia,--
OLIVIA
What do you say, Cesario? Good my lord,--
VIOLA
My lord would speak; my duty hushes me.
OLIVIA
If it be aught to the old tune, my lord,
It is as fat and fulsome to mine ear
As howling after music.
DUKE ORSINO
Still so cruel?
OLIVIA
Still so constant, lord.
DUKE ORSINO
What, to perverseness? you uncivil lady,

Twelfth Night — Act V

To whose ingrate and unauspicious altars
My soul the faithfull'st offerings hath breathed out
That e'er devotion tender'd! What shall I do?
OLIVIA
Even what it please my lord, that shall become him.
DUKE ORSINO
Why should I not, had I the heart to do it,
Like to the Egyptian thief at point of death,
Kill what I love?--a savage jealousy
That sometimes savours nobly. But hear me this:
Since you to non-regardance cast my faith,
And that I partly know the instrument
That screws me from my true place in your favour,
Live you the marble-breasted tyrant still;
But this your minion, whom I know you love,
And whom, by heaven I swear, I tender dearly,
Him will I tear out of that cruel eye,
Where he sits crowned in his master's spite.
Come, boy, with me; my thoughts are ripe in mischief:
I'll sacrifice the lamb that I do love,
To spite a raven's heart within a dove.
VIOLA
And I, most jocund, apt and willingly,
To do you rest, a thousand deaths would die.
OLIVIA
Where goes Cesario?
VIOLA
After him I love
More than I love these eyes, more than my life,
More, by all mores, than e'er I shall love wife.
If I do feign, you witnesses above
Punish my life for tainting of my love!
OLIVIA
Ay me, detested! how am I beguiled!

Twelfth Night — Act V

VIOLA
  Who does beguile you? who does do you wrong?
OLIVIA
  Hast thou forgot thyself? is it so long?
  Call forth the holy father.
DUKE ORSINO
  Come, away!
OLIVIA
  Whither, my lord? Cesario, husband, stay.
DUKE ORSINO
  Husband!
OLIVIA
  Ay, husband: can he that deny?
DUKE ORSINO
  Her husband, sirrah!
VIOLA
  No, my lord, not I.
OLIVIA
  Alas, it is the baseness of thy fear
  That makes thee strangle thy propriety:
  Fear not, Cesario; take thy fortunes up;
  Be that thou know'st thou art, and then thou art
  As great as that thou fear'st.

  Enter Priest

  O, welcome, father!
  Father, I charge thee, by thy reverence,
  Here to unfold, though lately we intended
  To keep in darkness what occasion now
  Reveals before 'tis ripe, what thou dost know
  Hath newly pass'd between this youth and me.
Priest
  A contract of eternal bond of love,
  Confirm'd by mutual joinder of your hands,

Twelfth Night — Act V

Attested by the holy close of lips,
Strengthen'd by interchangement of your rings;
And all the ceremony of this compact
Seal'd in my function, by my testimony:
Since when, my watch hath told me, toward my grave
I have travell'd but two hours.

DUKE ORSINO
O thou dissembling cub! what wilt thou be
When time hath sow'd a grizzle on thy case?
Or will not else thy craft so quickly grow,
That thine own trip shall be thine overthrow?
Farewell, and take her; but direct thy feet
Where thou and I henceforth may never meet.

VIOLA
My lord, I do protest--

OLIVIA
O, do not swear!
Hold little faith, though thou hast too much fear.

Enter SIR ANDREW

SIR ANDREW
For the love of God, a surgeon! Send one presently
to Sir Toby.

OLIVIA
What's the matter?

SIR ANDREW
He has broke my head across and has given Sir Toby
a bloody coxcomb too: for the love of God, your
help! I had rather than forty pound I were at home.

OLIVIA
Who has done this, Sir Andrew?

SIR ANDREW
The count's gentleman, one Cesario: we took him for
a coward, but he's the very devil incardinate.

Twelfth Night — Act V

DUKE ORSINO
 My gentleman, Cesario?
SIR ANDREW
 'Od's lifelings, here he is! You broke my head for
 nothing; and that that I did, I was set on to do't
 by Sir Toby.
VIOLA
 Why do you speak to me? I never hurt you:
 You drew your sword upon me without cause;
 But I bespoke you fair, and hurt you not.
SIR ANDREW
 If a bloody coxcomb be a hurt, you have hurt me: I
 think you set nothing by a bloody coxcomb.

Enter SIR TOBY BELCH and Clown

 Here comes Sir Toby halting; you shall hear more:
 but if he had not been in drink, he would have
 tickled you othergates than he did.
DUKE ORSINO
 How now, gentleman! how is't with you?
SIR TOBY BELCH
 That's all one: has hurt me, and there's the end
 on't. Sot, didst see Dick surgeon, sot?
Clown
 O, he's drunk, Sir Toby, an hour agone; his eyes
 were set at eight i' the morning.
SIR TOBY BELCH
 Then he's a rogue, and a passy measures panyn: I
 hate a drunken rogue.
OLIVIA
 Away with him! Who hath made this havoc with them?
SIR ANDREW
 I'll help you, Sir Toby, because we'll be dressed together.
SIR TOBY BELCH

Twelfth Night — Act V

Will you help? an ass-head and a coxcomb and a
knave, a thin-faced knave, a gull!
OLIVIA
Get him to bed, and let his hurt be look'd to.

*Exeunt Clown, FABIAN, SIR TOBY BELCH, and SIR
ANDREW*

Enter SEBASTIAN

SEBASTIAN
I am sorry, madam, I have hurt your kinsman:
But, had it been the brother of my blood,
I must have done no less with wit and safety.
You throw a strange regard upon me, and by that
I do perceive it hath offended you:
Pardon me, sweet one, even for the vows
We made each other but so late ago.
DUKE ORSINO
One face, one voice, one habit, and two persons,
A natural perspective, that is and is not!
SEBASTIAN
Antonio, O my dear Antonio!
How have the hours rack'd and tortured me,
Since I have lost thee!
ANTONIO
Sebastian are you?
SEBASTIAN
Fear'st thou that, Antonio?
ANTONIO
How have you made division of yourself?
An apple, cleft in two, is not more twin
Than these two creatures. Which is Sebastian?
OLIVIA

Twelfth Night — Act V

Most wonderful!
SEBASTIAN
Do I stand there? I never had a brother;
Nor can there be that deity in my nature,
Of here and every where. I had a sister,
Whom the blind waves and surges have devour'd.
Of charity, what kin are you to me?
What countryman? what name? what parentage?
VIOLA
Of Messaline: Sebastian was my father;
Such a Sebastian was my brother too,
So went he suited to his watery tomb:
If spirits can assume both form and suit
You come to fright us.
SEBASTIAN
A spirit I am indeed;
But am in that dimension grossly clad
Which from the womb I did participate.
Were you a woman, as the rest goes even,
I should my tears let fall upon your cheek,
And say 'Thrice-welcome, drowned Viola!'
VIOLA
My father had a mole upon his brow.
SEBASTIAN
And so had mine.
VIOLA
And died that day when Viola from her birth
Had number'd thirteen years.
SEBASTIAN
O, that record is lively in my soul!
He finished indeed his mortal act
That day that made my sister thirteen years.
VIOLA
If nothing lets to make us happy both

Twelfth Night — Act V

But this my masculine usurp'd attire,
Do not embrace me till each circumstance
Of place, time, fortune, do cohere and jump
That I am Viola: which to confirm,
I'll bring you to a captain in this town,
Where lie my maiden weeds; by whose gentle help
I was preserved to serve this noble count.
All the occurrence of my fortune since
Hath been between this lady and this lord.

SEBASTIAN
[To OLIVIA] So comes it, lady, you have been mistook:
But nature to her bias drew in that.
You would have been contracted to a maid;
Nor are you therein, by my life, deceived,
You are betroth'd both to a maid and man.

DUKE ORSINO
Be not amazed; right noble is his blood.
If this be so, as yet the glass seems true,
I shall have share in this most happy wreck.

To VIOLA

Boy, thou hast said to me a thousand times
Thou never shouldst love woman like to me.

VIOLA
And all those sayings will I overswear;
And those swearings keep as true in soul
As doth that orbed continent the fire
That severs day from night.

DUKE ORSINO
Give me thy hand;
And let me see thee in thy woman's weeds.

VIOLA
The captain that did bring me first on shore
Hath my maid's garments: he upon some action

Twelfth Night — Act V

Is now in durance, at Malvolio's suit,
A gentleman, and follower of my lady's.
OLIVIA
He shall enlarge him: fetch Malvolio hither:
And yet, alas, now I remember me,
They say, poor gentleman, he's much distract.

Re-enter Clown with a letter, and FABIAN

A most extracting frenzy of mine own
From my remembrance clearly banish'd his.
How does he, sirrah?
Clown
Truly, madam, he holds Belzebub at the staves's end as well as a man in his case may do: has here writ a letter to you; I should have given't you to-day morning, but as a madman's epistles are no gospels, so it skills not much when they are delivered.
OLIVIA
Open't, and read it.
Clown
Look then to be well edified when the fool delivers the madman.

Reads

'By the Lord, madam,'--
OLIVIA
How now! art thou mad?
Clown
No, madam, I do but read madness: an your ladyship will have it as it ought to be, you must allow Vox.
OLIVIA
Prithee, read i' thy right wits.
Clown

Twelfth Night — Act V

So I do, madonna; but to read his right wits is to
read thus: therefore perpend, my princess, and give ear.
OLIVIA
   Read it you, sirrah.

To FABIAN

FABIAN
   [Reads] 'By the Lord, madam, you wrong me, and the
   world shall know it: though you have put me into
   darkness and given your drunken cousin rule over
   me, yet have I the benefit of my senses as well as
   your ladyship. I have your own letter that induced
   me to the semblance I put on; with the which I doubt
   not but to do myself much right, or you much shame.
   Think of me as you please. I leave my duty a little
   unthought of and speak out of my injury.
      'THE MADLY-USED MALVOLIO."
OLIVIA
   Did he write this?
Clown
   Ay, madam.
DUKE ORSINO
   This savours not much of distraction.
OLIVIA
   See him deliver'd, Fabian; bring him hither.

Exit FABIAN

My lord so please you, these things further
thought on,
To think me as well a sister as a wife,
One day shall crown the alliance on't, so please you,
Here at my house and at my proper cost.
DUKE ORSINO

Twelfth Night — Act V

Madam, I am most apt to embrace your offer.
> *To VIOLA*

Your master quits you; and for your service done him,
So much against the mettle of your sex,
So far beneath your soft and tender breeding,
And since you call'd me master for so long,
Here is my hand: you shall from this time be
Your master's mistress.
OLIVIA
A sister! you are she.
> *Re-enter FABIAN, with MALVOLIO*

DUKE ORSINO
Is this the madman?
OLIVIA
Ay, my lord, this same.
How now, Malvolio!
MALVOLIO
Madam, you have done me wrong,
Notorious wrong.
OLIVIA
Have I, Malvolio? no.
MALVOLIO
Lady, you have. Pray you, peruse that letter.
You must not now deny it is your hand:
Write from it, if you can, in hand or phrase;
Or say 'tis not your seal, nor your invention:
You can say none of this: well, grant it then
And tell me, in the modesty of honour,
Why you have given me such clear lights of favour,
Bade me come smiling and cross-garter'd to you,
To put on yellow stockings and to frown

Twelfth Night — Act V

    Upon Sir Toby and the lighter people;
    And, acting this in an obedient hope,
    Why have you suffer'd me to be imprison'd,
    Kept in a dark house, visited by the priest,
    And made the most notorious geck and gull
    That e'er invention play'd on? tell me why.
OLIVIA
    Alas, Malvolio, this is not my writing,
    Though, I confess, much like the character
    But out of question 'tis Maria's hand.
    And now I do bethink me, it was she
    First told me thou wast mad; then camest in smiling,
    And in such forms which here were presupposed
    Upon thee in the letter. Prithee, be content:
    This practise hath most shrewdly pass'd upon thee;
    But when we know the grounds and authors of it,
    Thou shalt be both the plaintiff and the judge
    Of thine own cause.
FABIAN
    Good madam, hear me speak,
    And let no quarrel nor no brawl to come
    Taint the condition of this present hour,
    Which I have wonder'd at. In hope it shall not,
    Most freely I confess, myself and Toby
    Set this device against Malvolio here,
    Upon some stubborn and uncourteous parts
    We had conceived against him: Maria writ
    The letter at Sir Toby's great importance;
    In recompense whereof he hath married her.
    How with a sportful malice it was follow'd,
    May rather pluck on laughter than revenge;
    If that the injuries be justly weigh'd
    That have on both sides pass'd.
OLIVIA

Twelfth Night — Act V

Alas, poor fool, how have they baffled thee!
Clown
Why, 'some are born great, some achieve greatness,
and some have greatness thrown upon them.' I was
one, sir, in this interlude; one Sir Topas, sir; but
that's all one. 'By the Lord, fool, I am not mad.'
But do you remember? 'Madam, why laugh you at such
a barren rascal? an you smile not, he's gagged:'
and thus the whirligig of time brings in his revenges.
MALVOLIO
I'll be revenged on the whole pack of you.

Exit

OLIVIA
He hath been most notoriously abused.
DUKE ORSINO
Pursue him and entreat him to a peace:
He hath not told us of the captain yet:
When that is known and golden time convents,
A solemn combination shall be made
Of our dear souls. Meantime, sweet sister,
We will not part from hence. Cesario, come;
For so you shall be, while you are a man;
But when in other habits you are seen,
Orsino's mistress and his fancy's queen.

Exeunt all, except Clown

Clown
[Sings]
When that I was and a little tiny boy,
With hey, ho, the wind and the rain,
A foolish thing was but a toy,
For the rain it raineth every day.

Twelfth Night — Act V

But when I came to man's estate,
With hey, ho, & c.
'Gainst knaves and thieves men shut their gate,
For the rain, & c.
But when I came, alas! to wive,
With hey, ho, & c.
By swaggering could I never thrive,
For the rain, & c.
But when I came unto my beds,
With hey, ho, & c.
With toss-pots still had drunken heads,
For the rain, & c.
A great while ago the world begun,
With hey, ho, & c.
But that's all one, our play is done,
And we'll strive to please you every day.

Exit

Biography

A Short Life of Edward de Vere, 17th Earl of Oxford

by Dr. Kevin Gilvary, President
The de Vere Society

He was born on 12 April 1550 at Castle Hedingham, his family's ancestral home. His father, John de Vere, 16th Earl, was Lord Great Chamberlain and attended the coronations of both Mary and Elizabeth Tudor. His mother was Margaret Golding. Edward was 11 when, in 1561, Queen Elizabeth visited Hedingham for four days of masques, feasting and entertainments. When his father died in 1562, young Oxford left to become, like Bertram in *All's Well that Ends Well*, a ward of the Crown under the guardianship of William Cecil, the Queen's private secretary (later Lord Burghley, Lord Treasurer). His mother married Charles Tyrrell and seems to have passed out of the boy's life. His sister Mary went to live with her stepfather and the siblings were not reunited for some years.

According to a curriculum in Cecil's own hand, Edward de Vere's daily studies included dancing, French, Latin, writing and drawing, cosmography, penmanship, riding, shooting, exercise and prayer. Edward de Vere showed a prodigious talent for scholarship from his early years, and we may ascribe his lifelong love of learning to the influence of two of his early tutors. The first was Sir Thomas Smith who was, perhaps, England's most respected Greek scholar and the former Cambridge tutor of Sir William Cecil. It was, no doubt, through Cecil's influence that Edward de Vere spent some time living in the household of Smith in his early years, during which time he spent about five months at Smith's alma mater, Queens' College, Cambridge. Smith was a scholar of widely varied interests – this was reflected in his 400-volume library, some of which is still extant at Cambridge. De Vere's other tutor was Laurence Nowell, who was not only an accomplished cartographer but was also England's premier scholar of Anglo-Saxon literature – it was Nowell who possessed the only known copy of *Beowulf*.

Another important influence on Edward de Vere's early studies was his maternal uncle Arthur Golding, an officer in the Court of Wards under Cecil, who is credited with the translation of Ovid's *Metamorphoses*, published in 1567, a book widely recognised as having a major influence on 'Shakespeare'.

Following on from his matriculation at Cambridge in November 1558, Edward was awarded an honorary MA by Cambridge during a Royal progress in August 1564, and another degree by Oxford University during a Royal progress in 1566. Edward de Vere then attended Gray's Inn to study law. One notable feature of the Elizabethan Inns of Court was a tradition of mounting dramatic productions and of hosting the various touring companies of players.

In 1570 he served in a military campaign in Scotland under the Earl of Sussex. By 1571, he was reported as a leading luminary of the Court and, for a time, a favourite of Queen Elizabeth. In December 1571 he married Anne Cecil, aged 15, daughter of his guardian. This was a dynastic marriage where all the advantage accrued to Cecil who, ennobled as Baron Burghley, had reduced the social gap between himself and the young Earl.

While Oxford was away on a Grand Tour of Europe, he heard that his daughter Elizabeth Vere had been born in July 1575. On his return in early 1576, he appeared to have been convinced that Elizabeth was not his child; consequently he became estranged from Anne for five years, and exiled himself from Court, taking up residence in the Savoy and concerning himself with literary and musical patronage.

Already, in 1573, *Cardanus Comfort* (the Consolations of Boethius) had been translated from Latin by Thomas Bedingfield and dedicated to Oxford; and published with a preface written by him. In 1576 an anthology, *A Paradise of Daintie Devices*, including several poems by Oxford, was published. These are juvenile works but already show affinities, in both style and thought, with those of the mature Shakespeare.

Oxford's Grand Tour had taken in Paris, Strasbourg, Venice, Genoa, Florence, Palermo and, on his way back through France, Rousillon – the setting for *Love's Labour's Lost*. Oxford spent the best part of a year travelling in Italy in 1576, and becoming involved with moneylenders. He came back to England fluent in Italian and well acquainted with the northern Italian cities, to be satirised by Gabriel Harvey as 'The Italian Earl'. On his way back his ship was attacked by pirates in the English Channel (cf. *Hamlet*). Fourteen of 'Shakespeare's' plays have Italian settings, in which he put his detailed knowledge of the country, beyond pure book knowledge, to good use.

1573 saw the birth of Henry Wriothesley, Earl of Southampton. Although history has not bequeathed to us any evidence of a direct relationship between the two men, in the relatively small world of the royal Court, they must have been acquainted with each other. The poems *Venus and Adonis* (1593) and *The Rape of Lucrece* (1594) were dedicated to Southampton. These were the first works to be published under the name 'Shakespeare' and for the next five years the records show the byline 'Shakespeare' to have been associated exclusively with these two poems. Plays under the name 'Shakespeare' did not appear in print until 1598, the year that Lord Burghley died.

In May 1577 Oxford invested in Frobisher's voyage in the ship *Edward Bonaventure*. Despite its name, the ship's voyage across the Atlantic in search of the North-West Passage lost money; consequently he was forced to sell three estates (cf. Hamlet's words 'I am but mad north-north-west' II.1.). In 1578 he invested in Frobisher's second expedition, which also lost money, forcing further sales of estates.

He was mentioned by Gabriel Harvey in an address to Queen Elizabeth in July 1578, as a prolific private poet and one 'whose countenance shakes spears'. In the same year John Lyly, Oxford's secretary, published *Euphues.The Anatomy of Wit*, followed in 1579 by *Euphues and his England*, dedicated to Oxford. These two books launched the fashion for 'Euphuism', a style characterized by high-flown language, satirized in *Love's Labour's Lost*.

In March 1581 Oxford's mistress, Anne Vavasour, who was one of Queen Elizabeth's Ladies of the Bedchamber, gave birth to a son. The lovers and their son were sent to the Tower by an infuriated Queen but swiftly released (cf. *Measure for Measure*). After his release, Oxford was wounded in a street-fight provoked by Thomas Knyvet, a kinsman of Anne Vavasour; affrays continued in the streets of London between the rival gangs of supporters for over a year (cf.*Romeo and Juliet*).

In December 1581 he resumed living with his long-suffering and devoted wife, and accepted Elizabeth

Vere as his child. Tragically, their only son died one day after his birth. Three more daughters followed, of whom Susan and Bridget survived.

In 1584, Robert Greene's *Gwydonius; the Card of Fancy* was dedicated to him, identifying him as a 'pre-eminent writer'. In 1586, when he was 36, he served on the tribunal which condemned Mary, Queen of Scots to execution.

In the same year, the Queen awarded Oxford an unconditional pension of £1,000 a year for life (about £500,000 at today's value). The motive for this uncharacteristic generosity on the part of the Queen remains a mystery – no accounting was required of Oxford. Her successor, King James I, continued to pay the pension. In reply to Sir Robert Cecil's request that Lord Sheffield's pension be increased, the King refused, saying, 'Great Oxford got no more . . .', leaving us to wonder why Great Oxford? His greatness does not seem to have resided in war or any of the known offices of State. Perhaps a clue can be found in a letter to Burghley, written in 1594, in which Edward de Vere seeks his favour in a matter involving what he describes as 'in mine office' and that this office is beholden to the Queen.

In 1589, George Puttenham published *The Arte of English Poesie* and this contains the most telling recognition of Edward de Vere's literary standing amongst his contemporaries: 'And in her Majesties time that now is are sprong up an other crew of Courtly makers Noble men and Gentlemen of her Majesties owne servantes, who have written excellently well as it would appear if their doings could be found out and made publicke with the rest, of which number is first that noble Gentleman Edward Earle of Oxford.'

In 1588 his wife Anne, daughter of Lord Burghley, died and in extant letters written at this time, it is reported that Burghley is so incapacitated by grief over the death of his favourite daughter that he is incapable of conducting any Privy Council business.

Three years later, in 1591, Oxford married another of the Queen's Maids of Honour, Elizabeth Trentham, with whom he finally became the father of a male heir; Henry de Vere, 18th Earl of Oxford. Although there is evidence of his continued involvement in Court affairs, from the date of this marriage Edward de Vere's life at his new home at King's Place in Hackney is perhaps the most obscure of his entire life.

In 1594, his ship the *Edward Bonaventure* was wrecked in Bermuda (cf. *The Tempest*). In January 1595, Elizabeth Vere married William Stanley, 6th Earl of Derby, another literary earl who maintained his own company of players – many scholars believe that *A Midsummer Night's Dream* was written for these festivities which were attended by the whole royal Court.

On September 7 1598, Francis Meres' *Palladis Tamia* was registered for publication, naming Oxford as the 'best for comedy'. This is a vital document in Shakespearean history because it includes the first mention of 'Shakespeare' as a playwright, attributing twelve plays to him; until then Shakespeare's reputation had rested on the two narrative poems only.

Oxford suffered all his life from financial difficulties, much of which can be traced to the fact that Queen Elizabeth handed out the bulk of his estate to her favourite courtier the Earl of Leicester during Oxford's minority as a royal ward (estates which Oxford found almost impossible to reclaim), and the ruinous debt she placed upon him over his marriage to Anne Cecil. It is, however, notable that his new brother-in-law, the wealthy Staffordshire landowner and Knight of the Shire Francis Trentham, took over the management of Edward de

Vere's near-bankrupt estate from 1591 and gradually nursed it back to health so that, when Oxford died, all of his massive debts had been cleared.

On the Queen's death in 1603 Oxford wrote eloquently to Sir Robert Cecil, son and heir of Lord Burghley, of his 'great grief'. He wrote, 'In this common shipwreck, mine is above all the rest, who least regarded, though often comforted, she hath left to try my fortune among the alterations of time and chance'.

Oxford died in Hackney in 1604, cause unknown. Parish records state that he was buried in Hackney Church on July 6, but a family history by his first cousin Percival Golding, states 'Edward de Veer ... a man in mind and body absolutely accomplished with honorable endowments ... lieth buried at Westminster'. No record of such a burial can now be traced in Westminster Abbey, where there is a Vere family tomb.

The Aftermath of Oxford's life and death

During the winter season 1604-05, six of Shakespeare's plays were presented at Court by command of King James I. This has an air of commemoration. In 1609 the *Sonnets* were published in a pirated edition. The famous dedication describes the author as 'our ever-living', a phrase invariably used only of the dead.

In 1622 Henry Peacham published, in *The Compleat Gentelman*, a list of poets who made Elizabeth's reign a 'golden age'. Unaccountably, he omitted Shakespeare but placed the Earl of Oxford in first place in his list – perhaps he knew them to be the same person. This is unlike Meres who included them both – maybe one reason was because he didn't know Oxford and Shakespeare were the same person.

We do not know who instigated publication of the First Folio Edition of the Shakespeare plays in 1623, but there is no mention of any executor or relative of Shakspere of Stratford in connection with it. However, of the two brothers who financed it and to whom it was dedicated, one – Philip Earl of Montgomery – was the husband of Oxford's daughter Susan, while the other – William Earl of Pembroke – had once been a suitor for her sister Bridget. Pembroke was Lord Chamberlain, the supreme authority in the world of theatre, and thus in a position to decide which plays were to be published and which suppressed. We also know that Ben Jonson, who wrote much of the introductory material, was an intimate associate of the de Vere family after Oxford's death. The First Folio was therefore very much a family affair, but the family was not the one in Stratford-on-Avon.

An AfterVerse

For those with yet an interest
In strenuous debate
We've compiled a list of books and films
Your appetite to sate.
From this study clear your mind
Of doubt and all misgiving-
Who from us has long since gone
And who is ever-living.

Selected References & Bibliography
About the Author
Edward de Vere, 17th Earl of Oxford
Books

♦ Anderson, M. (2005). *Shakespeare by Another Name: The Life of Edward de Vere, Earl of Oxford, The Man who was Shakespeare.* New York: Gotham Books.
--*A physicist by training with research interest in how evidence supports or negates a theory, Mark Anderson spent ten years investigating Edward de Vere as the author of Shake-speare's works.*

♦Farina, William. (2006). *De Vere as Shakespeare: An Oxfordian Reading of the Canon.* Jefferson, NC. McFarland & Company.

--Each of the plays and poems is individually assessed and explored in its own chapter, using the innumerable connections between the text itself and the life of its author, Edward de Vere.

♦ Looney, J. Thomas (2018). *Shakespeare Identified.* Cary, N.C. Veritas Publicaations.
--First published in 1920 this book began the modern Oxfordian movement. From reading it, Sigmund Freud became convinced and John Galsworthy called it "the best detective story I ever read."

♦ Ogburn, C. (1992). *The Mysterious William Shakespeare.* McLean (Va.): EPM.
--An in depth exploration and must read foundational book on the authorship question.

♦Sobran, Joseph. (1997). *Alias Shakespeare: Solving the Greatest Literary Mystery of All Time.* New York; The Free Press, A Division of Simon & Schuster.
--A concise exploration of the puzzling questions surrounding the authorship controversy with the evidence decisively supporting the case for Edward de Vere, the 17th Earl of Oxford, as the rightful author of the Shakespeare plays and poems.

♦Whittemore, Hank. (2016), *100 Reasons Shake-speare Was the Earl of Oxford.* Somerville MA. Forever Press.
▶ Also with further discussion and public comment at: *Hank Whittemore's Shakespeare Blog.*
https://hankwhittemore.com/
--In both the book and online blog cited above, Whittemore presents a concise introduction to the

authorship question that examines 100 different aspects, from biographical and historical records, that point to Edward de Vere as the true writer of the Shake-speare plays and poems.

Websites & Videos

▶ De Vere Society. (2019). The de Vere Society – Dedicated to the proposition that the works of Shakespeare were written by Edward de Vere, 17th Earl of Oxford. [online] Deveresociety.co.uk. Available at: https://deveresociety.co.uk
--A very complete resource with substantial biographical and authorship information and links.

▶ The Oxford Fellowship (2019). Shakespeare Oxford Fellowship | Research and Discussion of the Shakespeare Authorship Question. [online] Shakespeare Oxford Fellowship. Available at: https://shakespeareoxfordfellowship.org/
--A seminal online resource especially focusing on the authorship question.

▶ Waugh, A. (2019). Alexander Waugh. [online] YouTube. Available at: https://www.youtube.com/channel/UCHN7SCKlsa9lPYJmqqQ2uIg/featured/
OR simply search: 'Alexander Waugh'
--Alexander Waugh is a leading authorship scholar who has produced many fascinating video presentations on the authorship question. This link is to his YouTube Channel.

▶ Columbia Pictures & Centropolis Entertainment. (2011). *Anonymous.* Produced and directed by Roland Emmerich. [DVD]
--*This mainstream film is both entertaining and enlightening. It presents a superb dramatization of the character of Edward de Vere, setting out in detail the historical and personal context which made his anonymous authorship necessary.*

▶ Centropolis Entertainment and First Folio Pictures. *Last Will and Testament.* (2012). [DVD]
--*A thoughtful and ground-breaking video documentary introduction to the Shakespeare authorship question.*

Acknowledgment
Our sincere thanks to
The de Vere Society
and
The Shakespeare Oxford Fellowship
for their inspiration, help and support in creating this series.

Attributions
--Character list from Wikipedia under the Creative Commons License 3.0
--Play text from the Moby(tm) editions in the public domain

Photos

Coat of Arms of Edward de Vere
Source: Wikimedia.org
Author: George Baker / Public domain

The Keep at Castle Hedingham
Source: geograph.org.uk
Author: David Phillips / CC BY-SA 2.0

The de Vere Family Coat of Arms
Source: Wikimedia
Author: Rs-nourse / CC BY-SA 3.0
(https://creativecommons.org/licenses/by-sa/3.0)

View from The Minstrels' Gallery, Hedingham Castle
Source: geograph.org.uk/p/3162585
Photo by: © PAUL FARMER - cc-by-sa/2.0

Cover/Inside: The Welbeck portrait of Edward de Vere (1575). Artist unknown. National Portrait Gallery, London.

This work has been edited and produced by

Verus Publishing
www.verusbooks.com

www.ingramcontent.com/pod-product-compliance
Lightning Source LLC
Chambersburg PA
CBHW030420100426
42812CB00028B/3038/J